Intervention Annotated Teacher's Edition

Marsha Roit
Marcy Stein

Level 4

A Division of The McGraw·Hill Companies

Columbus, Ohio

www.sra4kids.com

SRA/McGraw-Hill

A Division of The **McGraw·Hill** *Companies*

2005 Imprint

Copyright © 2002 by SRA/McGraw-Hill.

Send all inquiries to:
SRA/McGraw-Hill
8787 Orion Place
Columbus, OH 43240-4027

Printed in the United States of America.

ISBN 0-07-571045-5

5 6 7 8 9 QPD 06

Table of Contents

Worksheets

Jo

by Tara McCarthy

When I was younger, my family and I moved a lot. My sister, Sam, had a difficult time making friends. She was shy and scared to meet new people. One day after we had moved to a new town, Sam told me she had a new friend named Jo. But the problem was, Jo was an imaginary character from her favorite book.

"You should have *real* friends," I said to Sam. "Characters from books aren't real."

Sam said, "But Jo *is* real! She is my best friend. I have more fun with her than I do with anyone else. She and her family were pioneers more than 100 years ago. She has long brown hair and wears a dress and a bonnet on her head."

"If she lived more than 100 years ago, how can you see her now?" I said.

"I don't know," Sam said. "But she is a good friend. We play and talk by the pond in the backyard."

Sam was very young back then. Since I was her big brother, I took care of her a lot. I wanted her to be happy with real friends, not imaginary ones. So I took her to the playground to help her meet the other children in the neighborhood.

17
28
41
54
64
66
76
80
94
107
118
129
142
145
158
166
178
193
204
214

"Here are May and Ben," I said. "Why don't you play with them?" — 225 / 227

"Can Jo play, too?" Sam asked. — 233

May and Ben looked all around them. "Who is Jo?" they asked at the same time. — 244 / 249

I was starting to get annoyed at Sam, so we quickly left the park and walked home together. — 262 / 267

"Sam, no one else will be able to see and play with Jo," I said. "She isn't real." — 281 / 285

Sam sat down and looked at me. She always counted on me to tell her the truth. "OK," she said sadly. "I'll just have to tell Jo that I can't play with her anymore." I guess it's time I made new friends. — 297 / 311 / 325 / 327

The next day, Sam played with May and Ben. Sam said nothing more about Jo, and it made me happy to see her play with real children. — 338 / 351 / 354

I felt so great that night! I thought I had helped Sam grow up. Suddenly, I heard a strange voice in the backyard. I jumped out of bed and looked out the window. A little girl wearing a dress and a bonnet on her head was standing by the pond. It was Jo. — 367 / 379 / 392 / 405 / 407

I heard her say quietly, "You're a good brother. You helped your sister make new friends." Then Jo disappeared. — 418 / 426

As I look back, I understand I wasn't the only one who helped Sam. Jo was a friend to Sam when she really needed one. — 437 / 449 / 451

Dr. Jekyll's Other Self

Adapted from *The Strange Case of Dr. Jekyll and Mr. Hyde*

by Robert Louis Stevenson

Mr. Utterson had been Dr. Henry Jekyll's friend and lawyer for many years. One day, Dr. Jekyll visited Mr. Utterson to make out a strange new will. In case he disappeared, he said, he wished to leave all he owned to a certain Mr. Hyde.

This shocked Mr. Utterson. The few people who had ever met Hyde thought him repulsive. Hyde was not scarred or deformed in any way. But he had an ugliness that seemed to come from within. Perhaps Hyde knew a bad secret from Jekyll's past; perhaps he had threatened to reveal it unless Jekyll wrote this new will. Utterson could only guess.

Time passed. Rumors of evil deeds and wicked crimes committed by the hideous Mr. Hyde spread through the streets of London. Mr. Utterson begged Jekyll to think it over and change his will. But Jekyll was adamant; the will would not be altered.

All seemed well with Jekyll for some time after that. Then one night, Poole, one of Jekyll's servants, burst into Mr. Utterson's home. Dr. Jekyll had been locked in his laboratory for more than a week! People had heard odd sounds and a strange voice coming from the laboratory. He swore it wasn't Jekyll's voice. Poole feared Jekyll was in danger.

29

41

53

64

74

84

96

106

116

125

134

144

155

166

168

179

189

199

211

221

229

Alarmed, Utterson rushed to Jekyll's house with Poole. 237
Pounding on the laboratory door, Utterson demanded that it 246
be opened. The lawyer was shocked to hear Mr. Hyde's voice 257
inside. What had happened to Dr. Jekyll? 264

Outraged, and fearing for his friend, Utterson helped Poole 273
break down the old wooden door. A terrible sight greeted them. 284
On the floor Mr. Hyde lay dying, clutching the empty glass vial. 296
Dr. Jekyll was nowhere in sight. 302

Then Mr. Utterson noticed a letter on a desk not far from 314
Hyde's body. The letter was from Dr. Jekyll. It said: 324

The good and bad sides of the human nature have 334
intrigued me always. I chose early in life to follow the good 346
side of my nature. But by chance, while experimenting, I 356
found that I could separate the bad part of me from the good. 369
The temptation to do this was too great to resist. One night 381
I concocted a mixture of a white salt that I bought from the 394
chemist and a blood red liquid. I watched as the mixture 405
boiled and smoked in the glass. When the bubbling subsided, 415
I gathered my courage and swallowed the potion. 423

Suddenly I was in torment. A fierce feeling that I cannot 434
describe took over. Then swiftly these horrors were gone. 443
There was something strange about my body. I felt younger 453
and smaller. And I felt wicked—ten times more wicked than 464
I ever had before. Quickly I went to a mirror. With wonder, 476
I saw for the first time the face of Edward Hyde! 487

I began to drink the potion often to learn more about my 499
bad self. But soon I lost control. I would become Mr. Hyde 511
without even drinking the potion. I had trouble changing back 521
to Jekyll. Hyde took control of my body and all my deeds. 533

I have become frightened that one day I will disappear 543
forever and only Hyde will remain. 549

Mr. Utterson looked at Hyde's corpse and the few drops of 560
potion in the vial. He guessed that the few drops of potion in 573
the vial had killed Mr. Hyde. Alas, it has killed his good friend 586
Dr. Jekyll as well. 590

The Strange Case of Dr. Jekyll and Mr. Hyde is one of 602
Robert Louis Stevenson's best-known stories. Sometimes we 609
hear someone called a "Jekyll and Hyde." That means that the 620
person has a nature that changes greatly from one time to the 632
next. One day he may be warm and friendly. Another time he 644
may be unpleasant. You can never be sure how he may act. 656

A Snowman for Moose

by Carol Dornfeld Stevenson

4

8

Moose looked sadly through the window. Moose wasn't a moose. He was just a very big, very ugly dog. So he had been named Moose.

Moose was unhappy because his friend Timmy was lost. Timmy was a good boy, as boys go. But he did like to wander.

That was fine as long as Moose was with him. Moose could push him back into the yard and keep him safe. But today Timmy had gone out to play in the snow alone.

"You have to stay in, Moose, because you always knock down my snowmen!" Timmy had said. He was right. Moose loved the crunch when he pushed down a snowman.

Now Timmy was gone! His snowman was standing there, but Timmy was gone. And it was snowing very hard.

Where was he?

Timmy's mother looked down the road. Timmy's father looked up the road.

Moose slipped out, unnoticed. He didn't even look at the snowman. He headed straight for the woods. He was going to find Timmy!

17
31
33
42
56
68
80
90
100
110
119
128
138
141
149
153
163
174
176

Moose was sure Timmy was somewhere in the snowy   185
woods. He searched through the trees and bushes. But Timmy   195
wasn't there.   197

Moose pushed on into the field on the other side of   208
the woods. He sniffed all the drifts of snow. But Timmy   219
wasn't there.   221

Moose plodded on across the field. He could almost see the   232
old barn at the far edge of the field. Maybe Timmy was there,   245
hiding from the storm.   249

He was!   251

Moose jumped up and down and barked with joy. Timmy   261
was safe! Moose led him home through the snow.   270

"I lost my way in the snow," Timmy explained to his parents.   282
"But Moose got me home O.K.!"   288

The next morning it had stopped snowing. The snowman   297
was still there.   300

"Come on, Moose!" Timmy yelled. "Let's go out and knock   310
over that snowman!"   313

No Pets Allowed!

by Kathy Wong

3
6

Mrs. Crocker didn't like living all alone. A pet would
be good company, she thought. But the landlord, Mr. Glumly,
had put signs everywhere in the apartment building:
No Pets Allowed!

"How about one bird?" Mrs. Crocker asked Mr. Glumly
one day.

Mr. Glumly pointed to the sign. "No pets means no pets! If I
let you have one bird, someone else will want three birds!"

"How about a turtle?" Mrs. Crocker asked.

"No pets of any kind allowed!" Mr. Glumly said. "If I let you
have one turtle, someone else will want four turtles!"

One morning Mrs. Crocker saw this ad in the newspaper:
The Lucky Animal Shelter needs your help! Be a kind friend
to animals at the shelter and give them some time. Walk the
dogs. Pet the cats. Sign up today!

"That sounds like fun!" Mrs. Crocker thought. So she went
to the animal shelter and signed up. Then she walked a dog
named Penny. She petted ten cats. A puppy gave her a lick on
the face. A kitten sat in Mrs. Crocker's basket. But Mrs. Crocker
couldn't play with all of the dogs and cats at the animal shelter.
The shelter needed more funds and volunteers. Mrs. Crocker
wondered how else she could help.

16
26
34
37
46
48
61
72
79
92
101
111
122
134
141
151
163
176
188
201
210
216

When she got back home, she saw Mr. Glumly in the hall.   228

"Guess what!" Mrs. Crocker said to him. "I have a dog and   240
six kittens."   242

Mr. Glumly looked into the apartment. Of course, no pets   252
were there. "Very funny!" Mr. Glumly said.   259

Mrs. Crocker's next-door neighbor told her that she was   269
lonely and would love to have a pet also. So Mrs. Crocker   281
brought her to the shelter the next day to visit the animals.   293

The workers at the shelter said, "How will we find homes   304
for all of these animals?"   309

"No problem!" said Mrs. Crocker. "I'll call some of my   319
neighbors. I'll tell them about the shelter." Mrs. Crocker found 329
some more volunteers. She ran into Mr. Howell at the market.   340
He suggested that the shelter have a fund-raiser at his store   351
in the mall. They could raise money and find homes for   362
the animals.   364

Mrs. Crocker helped the shelter organize the fund-raiser.   372
She took pictures of the dogs and cats who needed homes. The   384
fund-raiser was a success. The shelter found homes for many of   395
the dogs and cats and raised a lot of money to help even more   409
animals in the future.   413

Mrs. Crocker felt happy that she could help the shelter.   423
Now she had many pets at the shelter to play with and keep   436
her company. And she hadn't even broken a single one of   447
Mr. Glumly's rules.   450

The Woodsman and the Ax

by Rosalie Koskenmaki

5

8

In a deep, dark woods of long ago, a man sat on a rock next
to a small pool, weeping. He seemed to be a poor man, for he
was not well-dressed. And his hands looked as though they had
known hard work. As he sat there on the rock, he felt very sad
and tired.

"Why do you weep?" asked a voice.

The man looked up. There in front of him stood a tall
stranger. He was dressed in fine silk clothes. And he had a very
kind face.

The weeping man spoke. "I am but a poor woodsman. I have
lost my ax, and I can do no work. My wife and children will not
have enough food."

The stranger softly spoke a single word. A beautiful gold ax
rose out of the pool. "Is this your ax?" the stranger asked the
woodsman.

"Oh, no. I'm sorry to say that is not my ax," the woodsman
answered.

23
37
48
62
64
71
83
96
98
110
125
128
139
152
153
166
167

The stranger said the word again. This time, a silver ax rose   179
out of the pool. "Is *this* your ax?" he asked the woodsman.   191

Again the woodsman answered sadly. "No, but thank you for   201
your trouble."   203

Then the stranger brought up the woodsman's own ax. "Yes,   213
yes," he cried. "That's it."   218

The stranger smiled at him. He said, "All three axes are   229
yours to keep." And he sent the woodsman off, singing a song   241
of joy.   243

Now a man who lived near the woodsman heard the story.   254
He wanted such good luck for himself. So he went and sat by   267
the pool. Soon he threw his ax into the pool and began to weep   281
loudly. The stranger came as before. The woodsman heard his   291
gentle voice. Then he saw the tall stranger standing in front of   303
him. The stranger asked why the man was weeping. The man   314
told him that he had lost his ax. It had fallen into the pool.   328

The stranger brought up an ax of gold. "Is this your ax?"   340
he asked.   342

The man cried, "Yes, yes. That is my ax!"   351

Upon hearing this, the stranger threw the gold ax back into   362
the pool. He drove the man away. And this time the man cried   375
real tears. Now he had no ax at all!   384

Sarah and the Appaloosas

by Olivia Berkhart

In 1877, I lived on a farm in Idaho with my mother, father, and sister, Sarah. We lived in Westlake. Our farm was on the banks of the Salmon River. Our town was near where the borders of Idaho, Oregon, and Washington meet. It's a beautiful world of rolling hills.

One day I went fishing with my sister. Not far down the river, we saw a young Native American boy. We knew he was from the Nez Perce ('nez-'pərs) tribe. Our father told us about the Battle at White Bird between the Nez Perce and the Army. He said that the army was escorting the Nez Perce to the reservation at Lapwai. Lapwai was just north of Westlake. A battle broke out between the soldiers and the Nez Perce. The Nez Perce wanted to return to their homeland in Washington. The Native Americans escaped on foot.

Just the day before, they were captured by soldiers. The soldiers rounded up their horses. Without horses, the Nez Perce could not escape. The Nez Perce bred horses called Appaloosas. They were faster and stronger and smarter than any horses the Army had.

My sister and I went over to where the boy was sitting. He looked at us. I told him my name was David. He told me his name was Wolf Dog. He and his people had been running from the army since the Battle of White Bird a few weeks earlier. They were very tired but would continue to run to keep their freedom. But Wolf Dog was very sad. He said that without Appaloosas, his people would no longer have a life worth living. They couldn't return to their precious homeland.

20
32
43
53
57
69
81
93
105
117
127
138
148
154
164
174
183
192
197
210
224
236
248
260
271
281
289

Sarah said our people were wrong to take the Appaloosas   299
away from the Nez Perce. She decided that we should help the   311
Nez Perce and free their horses. Then they could escape and   322
live where they wanted to live.   328

I didn't think that we could stop the Army, but Sarah   339
thought we could. She said we owed it to Wolf Dog because our   352
people took away their land. Then I got an idea.   362

Over 100 Appaloosas were corralled near town. There was a   372
passing circus camped there, too. They were going to open the   383
circus the next day. I had read in a flyer that the circus was   397
showing one of the first cars ever built, a Roper Steam   408
Carriage. They were going to charge people a nickel to see   419
somebody drive it around. Suddenly, I knew that a horseless   429
carriage would help us free the horses.   436

I found the car in one of the circus tents and got in it. I   451
started it up. It made a ton of noise. The soldiers came from all 465
over the town to see the car. They left the horses unattended.   477
They didn't hear Sarah and Wolf Dog free the horses until it   489
was too late.   492

The Nez Perce escaped before the soldiers knew what   501
was happening.   503

Canada's First Mapmaker

by Rosalie Koskimaki

When David Thompson was fourteen years old, he left his
home in Wales. He sailed to Canada.

That's not hard to do now, but David lived two hundred
years ago. It wasn't easy to sail across the Atlantic in
those days.

Canada was a new country. It had many forests, big rivers,
and high mountains. But there were not many people.

David loved this new country. It was so big! It was wild and
beautiful. There were many things to see. Although David was
blind in one eye, he looked at everything. The more he looked,
the more he loved the country.

David wanted to draw a map of Canada. It would show the
forests and the mountains. It would show the rivers and the
towns. Then people in other countries could see what Canada
was like.

David had to see all of Canada to make his map. He traveled
50,000 miles! Sometimes he rode horses. Sometimes he went in
boats. Most of the time he walked.

In the winter he was cold. In the summer he was hot.
Many times he was hungry and tired. But he worked on, year
after year.

David found rivers. He found mountains. He found forests   208
and towns. He put all these things on his map.   218

Finally the map was finished. It was the first map of Canada.   230

David's life was sad after that. He had no money left. He had   243
to sell his belongings. He even sold some of his clothes. Then   255
he found that he couldn't see at all anymore. He was   266
completely blind.   268

Everybody forgot what a good mapmaker he was. He was   278
all alone when he died.   283

But now David Thompson is famous. The Canadian people   292
have even put his picture on a stamp. They know now that he   305
was one of Canada's greatest explorers.   311

Li Chi and the Mermaid

by June Bodansky

Li Chi lived with her mother, her father, and her dog, Tiny, in a small house. The house stood between a mountain and a lake. The sea was also nearby.

Every morning, Li Chi would watch the sun rise over the lake. One spring morning she heard a voice.

"Please help me!"

She saw a woman swimming in the lake. "Who are you?" Li Chi asked.

"My name is Kai. I'm a mermaid," she said.

"What is a mermaid?" Li Chi asked.

"I am part woman and part fish. I live in the sea."

"Then why are you in the lake?" Li Chi asked.

"I got lost. I swam into a cave that led into the lake. Now the lake is angry because I swam in it. It won't let me leave. Please help me get back to my home in the sea."

"How can I help?" Li Chi cried.

"A white rose grows on top of the mountain. Fetch the rose, and bring it down here. If you throw the rose into the lake, it will let me go. The sea, too, is angry. It will flood the lake if I am not back tomorrow. The water will wreck your house."

Li Chi ran to tell her parents about the mermaid.

21
33
38
49
57
60
72
74
83
90
102
112
126
140
151
158
170
184
200
210
220

"We must find the rose," Father said. "We have to help the 232
mermaid, and we have to save our home." 240

"But, Father," Li Chi said. "Soon it will be dark. We will not 253
be able to see where we are going. Then a trip up the mountain 267
will be dangerous and unsafe." 272

"We must try. We must take the risk and rush up to the top 286
of the mountain," Mother said. "We cannot wait any longer." 296

Li Chi set off with Mother, Father, and Tiny. It was getting 308
dark. The climb up the mountain was hard. 316

At last they came to the top. But where was the rose? They 329
looked but did not see it. They searched but did not find it. 342

"What will we do?" Mother cried. 348

"Who will help the mermaid? Who will save our home?" 358
Father cried. 360

Then Tiny ran to a stone and began barking. Li Chi also ran 373
to the stone to check for the rose. A white rose grew behind it. 387
Li Chi cried with joy as she carefully picked the rose. 398

Slowly they climbed back down the mountain. It was dark 408
when they finally reached the bottom. Then Li Chi raced to the 420
lake and tossed in the rose. Kai waved goodbye as she swam 432
toward her home in the sea. 438

"We took a great risk, but we had to save our home. Now 451
we are all safe!" the family cried. They hugged each other. Then 463
they all gave Tiny a hug. 469

Rosa Parks Makes History

by Duncan Searl

Rosa Parks Is Arrested

On December 1, 1955, Rosa Parks boarded a bus for home after work. Little did she know her ride would go down in history.

At the next stop, some white riders boarded. One man had to stand. "Hey!" the bus driver called to Rosa. "Give this man your seat!" On the segregated buses of Montgomery, Alabama, white riders got seats first.

Rosa Parks did not move.

"Just give him the seat," the driver ordered.

The driver's yell did not disturb Rosa Parks. She stayed put. The more African-Americans in Alabama gave in, the worse they were treated.

"I'll have you arrested," the driver warned.

"You may do that," Rosa Parks replied gently.

At the next stop, two policemen rushed Rosa Parks off to the city jail.

11
21
33
35
46
58
67
72
77
85
96
105
108
115
123
134
137

African-Americans Protest

News of the arrest spread, and African-Americans got very angry. They had had enough of segregation. Lawyers persuaded Rosa Parks to become a test case. They wanted to prove that bus segregation was illegal. They would go all the way to the U.S. Supreme Court.

African-Americans boycotted the buses. They formed carpools, took cabs, rode bikes, walked; they did not ride the buses. A young minister in Montgomery led the boycott. His name was Martin Luther King, Jr.

Without African-American riders, the bus company lost money. So did businessmen along the bus routes. They tried to stop the boycott. African-Americans stood firm.

Segregated Buses Are Declared Illegal

After a year, news came from Washington. The Supreme Court justices agreed with Rosa Parks that segregated buses were illegal. All citizens have the right to ride the buses.

The rest is history. The Civil Rights Movement had begun. And Rosa Parks's case was the start of it all!

Two Different Rewards

A Folktale from Tibet

retold by Lloyd Anderson

On a high mountain lived two old men. The men were good
friends, but they were very different. One man was kind and
gentle. Taking care of his garden made him happy. The other
man was unhappy. All he thought about was getting rich.

One time the kind old man was working in his garden when
he found a small, injured bird. Feeling sorry for it, he took it
into his house. He did everything he could to make it well.
Finally, the bird recovered. The old man held it in his hand,
wished it well, and released it.

Before long, the man looked up in surprise, for the bird had
returned. Landing on the man's shoulder, the bird dropped a
seed into his hand. "Plant this seed," the bird said. "It is a very
special squash seed. Take good care of it, and you will be
rewarded."

The old man did as he was told. He planted the seed in
his best soil. Before long, a vine began to grow. Only one huge
squash grew on the vine. It grew into the biggest squash
the man had ever seen. It took five men just to carry it into
the house.

When the old man tried to peel the squash, he had a great   225
surprise. It was solid gold! Now the old man was very rich.   237
But he was still kind and good. He used his riches to help   250
anyone in need.   253

The old neighbor was jealous of his friend's riches. "Where   263
did you get that seed?" he demanded. The kind old man told   275
him about the bird.   279

The greedy old man went home. He got a bow and arrow   291
and hid behind a tree until he saw a little bird. Then he shot the 306
bird, breaking its leg. He pretended to be very sorry. He took   318
care of the bird until its leg had mended. Then he let it fly away. 333

Just as before, the bird returned and gave the man a seed.   345
"Plant this seed," the bird said. "It is a very special squash seed. 358
Take good care of it, and you will be rewarded."   367

The old man was excited. He planted, watered, and tended   377
the seed. Sure enough, a gigantic squash grew. This time it took   389
six men to carry the squash into the house.   398

The greedy old man waited until everyone left. He thought   408
about the reward the bird had promised. "I will be even richer   420
than my old neighbor," he thought. Then he got a sharp knife   432
and cut into the squash. He too had a great surprise! Instead of   445
gold, a big monster jumped out of the squash. The creature   456
lifted the old man right off the floor and shook him. "You are a   470
greedy old man. Shame on you!" the monster growled. He took   481
the man out and chased him into the forest. The man was never   494
seen again.   496

The magical bird had promised each man a reward. And   506
each man got the reward he deserved.   513

Two Tricky Friends

from Aesop's Fables

Fox and Stork were good friends. They saw each other often. But one day Fox played a trick on Stork.

He asked Story to dinner. Stork came and sat down at the table. Fox had made some soup. He put the soup into a low dish. This was fine for Fox. He could easily lap up the soup with his tongue.

But Stork had a long, thin bill. She could only get the tip of it in the soup. She tried and tried to get some soup. But she left the table as hungry as she could be.

Oh, how Fox wanted to laugh! He thought it was a very funny trick. But he kept a straight face.

"I am so sorry you did not like the soup," he said in a   138
sweet voice.   140

Stork was as nice as you please. "Oh, that is all right," she   153
said. "Please don't feel bad about dinner. Come and visit me   164
soon. Could you come to eat at my house next week?" Fox said   177
he would be very glad to come.   184

The day came. Fox went to visit Stork. They both sat down   196
at the table. Fox was very hungry. He planned to eat a lot. He   210
looked about for the food.   215

Stork brought in the dinner. She put it on the table. Fox   227
looked and became less happy.   232

The dinner was served in a jar with a very long neck. The   245
neck of the jar had a very small mouth. Stork could easily get   258
her long bill into the jar. She ate long and well.   269

Fox could not get his big mouth into the jar. He tried and   282
tried. But he could only lick the outside of the jar.   293

Stork turned to Fox and smiled sweetly. "I am sorry you do   305
not like the dinner," she said. "I think it is very good."   317

Since then foxes and storks have never been friends. But   327
both now know that no trick is funny if it means losing a friend.   341

A Peaceful Warrior

by Joan Dalin

3
6

Martin Luther King, Jr., was a great American hero because he fought for the rights of all Americans in a special way. Even when others used violence against him, he used only peaceful ways of fighting back. 16
29
39
43

Martin Luther King, Jr., was born on January 15, 1929, in Atlanta, Georgia. His father was a preacher. When the young King turned 18, he, too, became a preacher. Preaching helped King learn to use words to inspire people, one of his main talents. 53
63
73
85
87

He also read the works of Mahatma Gandhi. Gandhi was an Indian leader who had worked hard to create strong forms of peaceful protest. King was impressed with Gandhi's ideas. He resolved to use some of Gandhi's ways to help African-Americans. 97
108
117
128
129

Changing the Laws 132

Before laws were changed in the 1960s, life in the South was really hard and unfair for African-Americans. They could go to school only with other African-Americans. They could not eat in the same restaurant or stay in the same hotel with white people. They could ride only in the back of a bus. An African-American could not even drink from the same water fountain as a white person. 143
152
162
175
188
198
202

Martin Luther King, Jr., fought for equal rights for African-Americans through peaceful protest. One way he protested against discrimination was through boycotts. When people join together to refuse to use or buy something, they are participating in a boycott. From 1955–1956, King led a boycott of the buses in Montgomery, Alabama. 212
220
228
238
249
255

For a full year, African-Americans refused to ride the buses   265
in Montgomery. They wanted the right to sit anywhere on the   276
bus, just like white people. The boycott worked. On December   286
21, 1956, for the first time, African-Americans and whites sat   296
side by side on a Montgomery bus.   303

Peaceful Protests Work   306

Another kind of peaceful protest Martin Luther King, Jr.,   315
participated in is called a sit-in. During a sit-in, African-   325
Americans sat quietly in places marked "for whites only," such   335
as lunch counters, movie theaters, hotels, and libraries. King   344
was arrested during one of these sit-ins, although he soon was   355
released. Because of the sit-ins, new laws did away with the   366
"whites only" rule in many private places.   373

Another way King peacefully protested discrimination was   380
through demonstrations. In 1963, King held a number of   389
demonstrations in Birmingham, Alabama, to ban "whites only"   397
public property, such as drinking fountains, and to increase the 407
number of jobs for African-Americans. Many demonstrators   414
were arrested. Once again, King was among them. However, the   424
demonstrations worked. The Supreme Court ruled that   431
Birmingham's "whites only" rules were unconstitutional.   437

In 1963 the governor of Alabama tried to stop two African-   448
American students from signing up for classes at the University   458
of Alabama. In response, King led a march on Washington, D.C.   469
Two hundred and fifty thousand people of all races walked   479
together through the nation's capital. The march ended with   488
King's most famous speech: "I Have a Dream."   496

In 1964, at the age of 35, Martin Luther King, Jr., became the   509
youngest person ever to win the Nobel Peace Prize. He   519
continued to fight for the rights of all Americans until dying in 531
1968. In April of 1968, King was in Memphis, Tennessee,   541
supporting striking workers and was shot and killed.   549

The night before his murder, King gave a speech to a group   561
of protesters. He said, "I may not get there with you, but I want 575
you to know tonight that we as a people will get to the   588
promised land."   590

The New Mitt

by Kit Murphy

3
6

Lovida loved softball. "I'm going to be a pitcher," she told Ted. "One day, I'll be a famous ballplayer." 17
25

Ted was Lovida's next-door neighbor. Ted loved to play ball, too. "I'm a home-run hitter," said Ted. "Watch me knock the ball out of the park." 35
47
51

Ted had a new, red mitt. He had earned the money to buy it. He walked Mrs. Miller's dog. 65
70

Lovida wanted a new mitt, too. But she didn't have enough money. 80
82

"You can earn the money," said Ted. "Mrs. Green needs someone to walk her dog." 92
97

"But then I can't play ball," said Lovida. "Softball is fun. Walking dogs is boring." 108
112

One afternoon, Lovida went to get Ted. "Come on, Ted. Let's play ball," she called. 123
127

"I can't," answered Ted. "I'm walking dogs today. I'm earning money for a bat." 137
141

"Well, I want to play," said Lovida. "Let me borrow your new mitt." 152
154

"It looks like rain," said Ted. "I don't want it to get wet." 167

"Don't worry. Nothing with happen to it," promised Lovida. 176

Later, it began to rain. A crash of thunder frightened Lovida. 187
She ran home in a hurry. She left Ted's mitt at the ballpark. 200

The mitt was ruined. It was wet and dirty. Ted was upset. 212

"I'm sorry," said Lovida. "How can I get you a new mitt? I 225
don't have any money." 229

"You could walk dogs," said Ted. 235

"Then when will I play ball?" asked Lovida. 243

"We can play catch with the dogs," said Ted. 252

"That's a great idea," said Lovida. "We can earn money and 263
play ball at the same time. I can buy you another mitt. And 276
maybe I can get one for myself, too." 284

The Girl with Golden Hair

retold by Lynn Samuel

In days long ago, people did not know how to grow crops. In the spring and summer, people ate roots, bark, nuts, and leaves. But when winter arrived, they didn't have anything to eat. It was a very hard life!

One spring day, an old man lay sleeping under a tree. He and his people had gone hungry all winter. Now they were too tired and weak to look for food.

Suddenly, the old man woke up because he heard someone singing. He looked all around. At the edge of the woods stood a girl with golden hair.

The old man called to her. "Your voice is so comforting. It makes me happy."

The girl called back, "If you follow my instructions you will hear my voice forever. You will never go hungry again."

"I'll do whatever you say," said the old man.

"Here is a lock of my hair," said the girl. "Take it to the field beyond these trees. Let my golden hair brush the ground."

"What will this do?" asked the old man.

21
32
42
49
61
73
80
90
103
107
119
122
133
143
152
167
177
185

"Here is what will happen," said the girl. "Wherever my hair   196
touches, a new corn plant will spring up. Something like golden   207
hair will grow between the leaves. The plant will grow very tall.   219
By the end of the summer, the plant will feed you and your   232
people. But keep some of the seeds to plant next spring."   243

The girl gave the man a lock of her hair, then disappeared.   255

The old man did as he was told. He didn't go out with his   269
people to look for food. The old man tended his crop day after   282
day. He believed the girl's advice would help feed him and   293
his people.   295

Even though it didn't seem possible, everything happened   303
just as she said it would. Soon after the old man brushed the   316
field with the girl's hair, plants began to sprout. The corn grew   328
tall. The silk on the corn plants reminded the old man of the   341
girl with the golden hair.   346

The old man picked and cooked the corn over fire. He   357
shared it with his people. All winter long he and his people   369
had corn for food. The next spring, the old man and his people   382
planted the seeds. Again, the corn plants grew tall. They knew   393
they would never go hungry again.   399

One day as the old man was harvesting the corn, he heard   411
a young girl's voice carried by a soft breeze. It was the sweet   424
voice of the girl who taught him how to grow corn. Just as she   438
promised, he would hear her voice forever in his field of corn.   450

Hey, Peanuts!

by Mike Green

What a day Grant was having! Here he was at the baseball game. He should be having fun, but it was cool and damp outside. Wet leaves covered the seats. His dad had to work, so Grant had gone with his older brother. And his team was losing badly. At least he had money in his pocket. His mom had given him money to buy a snack.

Along came the popcorn man. "Popcorn! Popcorn!" he shouted.

"It's as if he's yelling right at me," thought Grant. The popcorn man also didn't seem to be having a good day. Grant decided to wait for something else.

"Hot dogs!" Grant heard. Here came the hot dog woman. Again, she barked, "Hot dogs! Doesn't anybody want a hot dog?" Grant didn't. No one else wanted one either.

Grant's stomach started making noises. He was really hungry. Then he heard, "Hey, peanuts! Get your peanuts! Invisible peanuts right here!"

Invisible peanuts? How could someone be selling invisible peanuts? Grant saw the peanut man walking his way.

"Hey, peanuts! Get your invisible peanuts!"

17
29
41
53
66
72
79
81
92
104
110
120
130
139
147
156
160
168
177
183

"How can they be invisible?" a woman wanted to know.   193

"Because they disappear!" the peanut man answered.   200
"Watch this!" He threw a peanut into the air and caught it in his   214
mouth. "Look, no more peanut!"   219

The woman laughed. "Here, I'll take a bag of those invisible   230
peanuts." She handed the peanut man some money.   238

The peanut man threw a bag of peanuts into the air. He   250
spun around and caught the bag before it dropped. Then, he   261
handed it to the woman and bowed. "Thank you, Miss." She   272
laughed again.   274

"Hey, I'll take a bag of peanuts, too," a man said. This time,   287
the peanut man threw a bag in the air and spun around twice.   300
He caught it behind his back and tossed it to the man.   312

Now everyone was crying out, "Hey, I'll take some peanuts!   322
I'd like some peanuts, too!" Grant shouted louder than anyone.   332
The peanut man tossed a bag high into the air. Then he jumped   345
up and gently batted the bag over to Grant.   354

"You're a great act," Grant said, catching the peanuts.   363
"No, I'm just a peanut man who loves my job!"   373

Puppy Problems

by Margaret Springer

Usually Maggie had to wait for her alarm to ring, but this 17
Monday morning she jumped right out of bed. She had been 28
planning for this day for weeks. Today was the grand opening 39
of Playful Puppy Day Care. 44

Maggie's dog, Crackers, jumped off her bed. "We've got a big 55
day today," Maggie said as she scratched his head. "Today is the 67
first day of our new business. You're going to have a lot of 80
friends to play with." 84

Maggie got the idea for her business from her neighbor, Mrs. 95
Boggs. Maggie walked Mrs. Boggs's dog every day because Mrs. 105
Boggs didn't get home from work until six o'clock. "I wish 116
Muffin wasn't alone all day," Mrs. Boggs often said. "I wish she 128
had other dogs to play with." 134

Other neighbors had the same problem. They just didn't 143
seem to have enough time for their pets. While Maggie was 154
thinking of how to spend her summer, her mother said, "Why 165
don't you see if some of the neighbors would like for you to 178
take care of their dogs during the day? We have a big yard, and 192
you could use the basement, too." 198

Maggie spent almost a month getting everything ready. She 207
and her mother went to yard sales and bought some old chairs 219
and rugs. She also collected dog toys, brushes, and leashes. 229
Then she made a flyer and posted it around the neighborhood. 240

Now, Maggie could hardly eat breakfast. She checked 248
everything again and again. Finally, it was nine o'clock, and 258
there was a knock at the door. 265

Mrs. Boggs and Muffin were waiting on the porch. "Hi, 275
Muffin!" Maggie said as she brought the dog inside. 284

As Maggie walked Mrs. Boggs to the door, she saw Mr. 295
Henry coming up the stairs with two tiny puppies behind him. 306
"Sammy and Pammy couldn't wait to come," he said. "Just don't 317
let them out of your sight." 323

Maggie gave the dogs some toys to play with as Muffin 334
watched from her chair. Before she could sit down, Maggie 344
heard another knock. Five more neighbors and their puppies 353
and dogs were waiting at the door. 360

As Maggie settled the dogs in the yard, she was almost 371
ready to cry. "Mom, I've got too many dogs," she said. "What 383
should I do?" 386

"I think you need a business partner," Mom said. "Why don't 397
you try calling one of your friends to help you?" 407

"You're right," Maggie answered. "Can you watch the dogs 416
while I call Ethan?" 420

A few minutes later, Maggie returned with a smile. "Ethan 430
can help me every day, and I'll pay him half of my earnings," 444
she said. "Now we're partners—with puppies!" 451

Who Is the Cleverest?

adapted from an Ethiopian folktale

retold by Pam Conrad

4

9

13

Many years ago, a clever man lived with his three sons. As
he grew old, he became ill and spent much of his time in his
room. During the day, his room had light from a small window.
But in the evening, the room was like walking in a forest on a
moonless night.

One day, the man called his three sons to him. He said, "I
wonder which of you has the gift of cleverness. I have decided
that my cleverest son will inherit my money." The sons looked
at each other and waited for their father to say more.

The father continued, "I will give each of you the same
amount of money. Use it to buy something to fill this room."
Each son took his money.

The oldest son thought, "This will not take long. I will go to
the market, since it is close by. I will find something there." At
the market, the oldest son bought the first thing he saw, which
was straw.

25

39

51

65

67

80

92

103

114

125

137

142

155

168

180

182

The second son thought about what would fill the room. 192
Then he, too, went to the market. As he looked he thought to 205
himself, "this is like looking for a needle in a haystack. It is 218
hard to find something for this amount of money that will fill 230
the room." But finally, he bought some feathers. 238

The youngest son went to a quiet place. He wanted to think 250
through his ideas undisturbed. He carefully thought about each 259
possibility. Finally, when he knew just what to buy, the third 270
son also went to the market. He bought two small items. He 282
wrapped them in a scarf and put them in his pocket. 293

At dusk, just as the sun was beginning to set, the father 305
called his three sons to him. "Show me what you have found to 318
fill my room," he said. 323

The first son stepped forward and quickly spread out 332
his straw. Sadly, everyone saw that the straw only filled one 343
corner of the room. Then, the second son threw out his 354
feathers. Sadly, everyone saw that the feathers only filled two 364
corners of the room. 368

"Hurry," the man said to his third and youngest son. "It is 380
growing dark. Did you find something that will fill my room?" 391

The youngest son came forward. He held two items in his 402
hand, covered with the scarf. He smiled as he slowly showed 413
his family what he had bought—a match and a candle. Then, he 426
used the match to light the candle. Instantly, the soft light filled 438
the room. 440

This pleased the father. The man said, "That is a fine idea. 452
You are my cleverest son! You inherit my riches. Use them 463
wisely to take care of yourself and your brothers, and you shall 475
be happy." 477

From Making Music to Making Food: Dreams That Change

by Joyce Mallery

Ever since he can remember, John Haskell wanted to make music. "I had to tell him to leave the piano, put on a coat, and play outside," his mother remembers. John liked to practice the piano when he was young, usually an hour a day.

"When I was lonely, I would play the piano," he said. "My mother didn't have to nag me."

John began taking piano lessons when he was five years old. By the time he was in middle school, he played the piano in church and in the school band.

When John was in high school, he began to dream of making a living by playing the piano. He played the piano for music groups and joined rock-and-roll bands.

No Longer a Dream

By the time John finished college, he was ready to make his dream a reality. And he did. He earned a living by playing the piano. He played in rock bands and played the organ at church. He gave piano lessons to children and played the piano for music groups. He also traveled to Japan, England, and Russia to play for opera groups.

"I loved it," he says. "I got to play wonderful music and meet lots of people. But it was also very hard work." He had to learn different kinds of music.

5
9
12
22
37
47
57
69
75
85
99
105
116
128
134
138
150
163
175
186
196
201
214
228
232

Changing Dreams 234

    As John got older, his dream began to change. "I played the 246
piano for over 30 years. It got harder to enjoy playing because I 259
did it so much. I wanted to do different kinds of music, more as 275
a hobby." 277

    So, another dream began to grow. John always loved to 287
cook and to try different kinds of food. His mother cooked for 299
other people, and his grandfather owned a restaurant. 307

    John decided to go back to school and become a chef. He 319
learned how to bake and cook for large groups. He 329
experimented with new kinds of food. He also had to learn how 341
to cook safely and to keep a clean kitchen. 350

    "I was 47 when I went back to school, and it was great!" he 364
says. "I loved learning something new and spending days in the 375
kitchen." He could also spend time writing his own music 385
instead of playing the piano to earn a living. 394

    Now John was ready to follow a new dream—to open his 406
own restaurant. "I want to cook interesting food for people," he 417
says. "I want to use fresh foods and to make food exciting." 429

    "People change," he says. "I found out that you can follow 440
many dreams during your life and make them come true!" 450

Intervention

Potato Chips—The Real Story

by Anna Newman

5
8
20
29
42
50
62
71
82
92
104
107
112
122
133
146
156
168
181
186

If you asked ten friends to name their favorite snack, quite a few might answer—potato chips! These thin, crispy potato slices are one of America's favorite snacks. We owe it all to a quarrel over how French fries should be prepared.

In the summer of 1853, George Crum worked as a chef in a restaurant in New York City. French-fried potatoes were on the menu. These thick potato slices were first popular in France. Then Thomas Jefferson brought the idea back with him after a visit there. Soon French fries were popular in the United States, too.

From Thick to Thin Potatoes

One evening, a diner at the restaurant where Crum worked didn't like his potatoes. He thought the French fries were too thick, and he sent them back to the kitchen. Crum cut them up and prepared another batch. But the customer still didn't like them. At this point, Crum got really angry. He then cut the potatoes so thin they couldn't be picked up with a fork and had to be eaten by hand.

Then guess what happened! The customer loved the chips! 195
Others wanted their potatoes exactly the same way. Soon Crum 205
quit his job and opened his own restaurant. His crunchy chips 216
were a huge success. 220

At Last, the Potato Peeler! 225

But it took a long time to cut and peel potatoes. Then the 238
potato peeler was invented in the 1920s. Now potatoes could be 249
cut much more quickly than before. Soon after, chips became a 260
top-selling food in New England. 266

Around the same time, a traveling salesman named Herman 275
Lay began to sell chips in the South. He sold the chips out of 289
the trunk of his car. This was the beginning of Lay's potato 301
chips, the first successful national brand of potato chips. 310

By the 1960s, new machines were being used to make 320
potato chips. They affected both the quality and quantity of 330
potato chips being produced. These machines also helped 338
change the potato chip business into an industry. 346

Today, chips come fried, baked, wavy, flat, spicy, and 355
barbecued. Machines peel, slice, fry, salt, and pack all the 365
potato chips we see in the store. And we keep those machines 377
busy! Americans now eat more potato chips than any other 387
people in the world. Thanks to George Crum, we can keep 398
on crunching. 400

The Shady Tree

adapted from a Chinese folktale

retold by Elizabeth Sengel

Long ago, there was a rich man who lived in China. A big   25
cypress tree grew in the rich man's garden, near the side of the   38
road. The tree had wide, green limbs that cast refreshing   48
shade. In the evening, the rich man liked to go outside after   60
supper to enjoy the shade and the cool breeze.   69

One day, a villager was passing by the rich man's house. He   81
was hot and tired from walking in the sun. He noticed the big   94
tree and sat down to rest under its green branches. When the   106
rich man saw him, he ran out of his house and ordered him   119
to leave.   121

"Why should I leave?" asked the villager. "I've done nothing   131
wrong. The road is public property. It's paid for by the   142
taxpayers."   143

"Yes," replied the rich man, "but the tree belongs to me. I   155
planted it and have been tending it for many years. I'm the only 168
one who can enjoy its shade."   174

"Well," said the villager, "will you sell me the shade?"   184

The idea of making some money pleased the rich man   194
greatly. "Yes," he agreed, "you may buy it."   202

The two men talked about the price, finally settling on an 213
amount. The villager paid the money. But he insisted that the 224
rich man give him a deed for the shade. 233

After that, the villager came by every day to sit under the 245
tree. Sometimes he brought his friends with him. They sat 255
themselves down wherever the shadow fell—in the courtyard, 264
in the kitchen, or even in the rich man's bedroom. 274

The rich man was beside himself with anger. One day, he 285
stormed out of the house and yelled, "What right do you have 297
to trespass on my property?" 302

The villager pulled the deed out of his shirt pocket. "I have 314
every right," he proclaimed. "I own the shade, and I can sit 326
wherever it goes." This annoyed the rich man so much that 337
he took the villager to court. He lost the case, however. The 349
villager's deed proved that the rich man had sold the shade 360
to him. And the villager could use his property however 370
he wished. 372

"How am I going to get rid of this person?" the rich man 385
wondered desperately. He asked to buy back the shade, but the 396
villager refused. 398

Not long after that, the rich man gave a big party. Many 410
people arrived, wearing fancy clothes and glittering jewels. The 419
villager and his friends, who were not dressed in fine clothes, 430
strolled into the house. They plopped themselves down in the 440
living room, where the tree's shadow had fallen. 448

"Who are those people?" the guests whispered. "What a 457
peculiar sight!" Then someone explained that their host had 466
sold the shade to the villager. The guests laughed and laughed, 477
retelling the story among themselves. Imagine someone so 485
foolish as to sell the shade of a tree! They had never heard 498
anything so funny. 501

The rich man soon became the laughingstock of the town. 511
He was so unhappy that he fled to another province. 521

As for the villager, he continued to enjoy the cool shade of 533
the tree. And he always invited anyone who was hot or tired to 546
rest under its wide, green branches. 552

The Story of Pretzels

by Lee Chang

Every year, food companies introduce new kinds of
pretzels. They include sticks and loops that are hard, soft,
thick, thin, plain, and salted. You can even choose cheese
pretzels if you like! But when were pretzels first produced?

The First Pretzels

The truth is that bakers have been making pretzels for over
1,500 years. Pretzels were probably first made by monks in
southern Europe in A.D. 610. They used scraps of dough left
over from bread to make the pretzels. They baked them as a
reward for children who learned their prayers. The pretzel's
twists were meant to look like the crossed arms of a child
praying.

Proof for this idea may be found in the word pretzel itself.
The Latin word *pretiola* means "small reward." This word was
probably the root for pretzel.

15
25
35
45
48
59
69
80
92
101
113
114
126
136
141

A Lucky Accident   144

    In time, pretzels grew in popularity due to an accident.   154
Originally, all pretzels were soft and chewy. Then, one   163
afternoon, a baker's helper fell asleep while watching an oven.   173
The pretzels inside were baked to a hard crisp.   182

    When the baker returned, he yelled at the helper and angrily   193
bit into the hard pretzel. To his great surprise, the baker found   205
that the flavor was actually better. He also enjoyed the crunch.   216
He gave the pretzels to his family, who consumed them with   227
delight. Soon, all bakers were producing hard pretzels.   235

Pretzels in America   238

    The first commercial pretzel bakery in the United States   247
opened in 1861 in the small town of Lititz, Pennsylvania. The   258
building there is still standing, more than 100 years later.   268

    Today, companies across America produce pretzels. The   275
pretzel makers keep coming up with more and more different   285
flavors to try. Pretzels remain one of the most popular snack   296
foods ever consumed.   299

The Queen's Shawl

by Eleanor Nicholson

Once there was a greedy queen. She had many jewels and   17
furs. She had four dresses for every day of the year. She had   30
shoes of gold and silver. She had everything. But she always   41
wanted something more.   44

One day the queen was looking for something to wear. She   55
looked in all the rooms of the castle. But nothing pleased her.   67
She picked up a shawl. It was a beautiful shawl. She had worn   80
it once or twice.   84

"I'm tired of this old thing," she said. She threw the shawl   96
out of the window. It fell on the back of a poor old woman who   111
was passing below.   114

A clever man saw this happen. He had an idea. He went up   127
to the old woman.   131

"I will give you five hundred gold coins for that shawl,"   142
he said.   144

Now that was a lot of money. The old woman gladly sold   156
the shawl. Then the clever man ran to the queen.   166

"Isn't this a lovely shawl, Your Highness?" he said. "It is for my wife." 178 180

The queen didn't realize that it was the same shawl she had thrown away. "It is lovely," she said. "I want it." 192 202

"I'm sorry," said the man. "You may not have it. It's for my wife." 214 216

"I *will* have it!" said the queen. "No," said the man. 227

No one had ever said *no* to the queen before. She was furious. 239 240

"YES!" she screamed. 243

"No," he answered quietly. 247

"I will give you half my jewels and half my furs. I will even give you my gold bicycle," said the queen. 261 269

"Oh, all right," said the clever man. 276

The queen gave him all she had promised. She put the shawl round her shoulders. "It's the most beautiful thing I ever saw," she said happily. 288 299 302

Isn't that a nice story? Everyone was happy. The clever man was happy. His plan had worked. He was a very rich man now. 313 326

The old woman was happy too. She had five hundred gold coins. She never had to work again. 337 344

Even the greedy queen was happy. It was the first time she had ever given anything up to get what she wanted. And that made her love the shawl very much! 356 367 374

Lucky Chuck

by Bonnie Nims

2
5

Clutching his box of samples, Chuck walked to the nicest 15
building on the block. He'd saved it for last. Its porch was 27
swept clean. Tubs of bright flowers were by the door. 37

Inside, the wooden stairs were waxed to a shine. Everything 47
looked clean and happy. The people here would be glad to buy 59
his greeting cards. 62

Chuck marched bravely up to the fourth floor. He knocked 72
at each door. But nobody answered. He walked down to the 83
third floor. 85

"No speak English," said a lady on three. Next Chuck talked 96
to an old man. But he shook his head sadly. "I've got no one to 111
send a greeting to." A woman with two crying babies said she 123
didn't even have time to think. 129

On the second floor, Chuck went from door to door tying 140
find someone at home. He knocked on a door and a dog 152
growled angrily. Then—*BAM!* The dog threw itself against the 162
thin wood door. 165

Chuck turned and ran. He slipped on the waxed stairs and bumped noisily down to the ground floor.

"What's going on?" asked a gruff voice. Then big strong hands pulled him up. "You all right, son?" The voice was kindly now.

Chuck nodded at a tall, white-haired man.

"What you got there?"

"Greeting cards."

"I thought so. My grandson sells them. He could sell ice cream at the North Pole."

Chuck tried to smile. "I couldn't sell *blankets!*"

"Me neither! But I *can* grow flowers and fix things. So I'm a caretaker. This is my building."

"It's the nicest one on the block." Chuck really smiled now.

The caretaker looked at him. "How'd you like a job helping me? My grandson's too busy selling—"

"I'd rather do that than sell a *million* cards!" Chuck said.

"O.K.! See you first thing tomorrow then."

Chuck waved and hurried out of the building, hoping that morning would hurry, too.

Market Day in Santa Fe

by Lauren Friedland

5

8

Every morning, Ann and Pablo walked to their school in   18
Santa Fe, New Mexico. Along the way, they passed the portal,   29
or front porch, of the Palace of the Governors. They admired   40
the colorful paintings, drawings, baskets, and pottery sold there   49
by Native American vendors. Every day, Native Americans from   58
all over New Mexico sold their arts and crafts at the market.   70

"I am proud of our school and the people in it," Ann said.   83
"Our school was founded by great artists like these. Artists   93
have always been a big part of Santa Fe. I hope it always stays   107
that way."   109

"I wish there were things in our school to help us learn how   122
to make arts and crafts like these," Pablo said.   131

At school, Ann and Pablo's teacher, Mr. Garcia, asked the   141
class what they would like to do for their class project. It took   154
them awhile, but they finally came up with an idea.   164

"Why don't we have our own market like the market at the   176
portal?" Pablo suggested to Mr. Garcia.   182

"That's an extremely interesting idea," Mr. Garcia said. "Why   191
do you want to have a market?" he asked them.   201

"To make money for things we want at our school," Pablo   212
said. "We would like to learn how to make arts and crafts like   225
those we see at the market every day."   233

All the students agreed they would like to learn how to   244
make traditional Native American arts and crafts.   251

"What would you like to sell at this market?" Mr. Garcia   262
asked.   263

Someone suggested they bake things like bread, cookies, and tamales. Someone else suggested they make items like beaded bracelets and necklaces. 271 280 284

Mr. Garcia called for everyone's attention. "This is great, but we have to have a plan. In order to make a profit, we need to consider a few things. How much will the supplies we need cost? How much will we charge for the things we sell? The cost of what we make subtracted from the price we charge for the items is our profit. This is the money we can use to set up an arts program at the school. We also need to think about advertising. If people do not know about our market, we will not make any money. Who would like to handle the advertising?" 294 309 320 333 345 360 371 382 392 393

The next few weeks were the best. Students made colorful posters and placed them around town. They also made and grew things for their market. Many students had friends, parents, or neighbors who wanted to help. 403 413 422 429

Soon, Student Market Day arrived. There were friendship bracelets and other student-made jewelry and food. Fruits, vegetables, and herbs were sold, too. The market was a success. The students were proud of the work they had done. 437 446 456 467

Today, there is a studio with a potter's wheel to make pottery and other things for artists in the school. Students now can learn how to make traditional Native American arts and crafts. 478 489 498 500

Sweet Success

by Shirley Beckmore

Has this ever happened to you? You're in the grocery store.   16
Something pulls you to the ice cream section. You can almost   27
taste a delicious ice cream cone. You can't stand it! A minute   39
later, you're begging your mom or dad to buy you your favorite   51
kind of ice cream. Maybe it's even the one made by two men   64
named Ben and Jerry in Vermont.   70

How Ben and Jerry Started Making Ice Cream   78

Ben Cohen and Jerry Greenfield both grew up on Long   88
Island in New York. They first met in junior high school in 1963.   101
They were the slow runners in their gym class. So they had   113
plenty of time to talk about their dreams. They each had the   125
same dream. They wanted to run a food business.   134

Later they decided to team up and go into the food   145
business. They both loved bagels. But the equipment to make   155
bagels cost $40,000. So they changed from bagels to ice cream.   166

Ben and Jerry learned how to make ice cream. To save   177
money, they bought some second hand equipment. They set   186
up an ice cream shop in Burlington, Vermont. They called it   197
Ben & Jerry's Homemade Ice Cream Parlour. The shop opened   207
for business in May 1978, in an old gas station in the center   220
of town. Soon the ice cream Ben and Jerry made was a big   233
success.   234

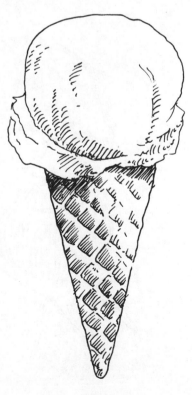

Dreams Can Come True

Now it is more than 20 years later. The ice cream is still popular. You can find it in almost any grocery store in the United States. Ben and Jerry keep making good ice cream. But they also do lots of good work for the community and the environment.

In 1985 they set up the Ben & Jerry's Foundation. Some profits from the company go into the foundation. Then the money is spent on various projects to help people and save the environment.

Jerry once said, "If it's not fun, why do it?" Ben and Jerry seem to have fun making their ice cream. And we're having lots of fun with the results!

Loyalty

by Ryerson Johnson

1

4

When the Hudson's Bay Company's trading post was robbed, everyone in the little Quebec town of Rolling River was certain who had done it: It was Carcajou André, of course! André was called Carcajou because, like the real carcajou, or wolverine, he was a trap robber. He stole the catch out of traps and didn't care whose traps they were.

But this time he had robbed more than traps; he had broken into the trading post warehouse and taken all the beaver furs that were waiting to be shipped.

Both Carcajou André and the furs had disappeared. Now it was a job for the Royal Canadian Mounted Police. The Mounties would find the thief. Didn't they always?

But Marie Lebrun hope they would not, for Marie knew two things that no one else knew. She knew where the furs were hidden, and she knew who the thief was.

After school Marie worked the traplines with her father and her older brother, Paul. Marie admired her brother and looked up to him. That was what made her discovery more heartbreaking.

12
23
34
44
57
64

76
87
93

103
113
121

132
144
152

161
171
182
183

Today it had been her turn to check the traps along Lost   195
Creek. A cold rain, together with an icy wind, drove her to a   208
cave, where she could make a fire and warm her wet feet. It   221
was a creekside cave where she and her brother had played as   233
children.   234

It was in the cave where Marie made her discovery. The   245
cave was filled with bundles of beaver furs—the bundles that   256
had been reported stolen.   260

Fresh boot marks were everywhere. They were made by   269
new boots, and Marie knew her brother had new boots. Then   280
Marie noticed something else. She bent down to pick up a   291
leather glove. Only last evening at the dinner table her brother   302
had mentioned losing his glove!   307

Marie was more confused and unhappy than she had ever   317
been in her life. She wanted to deny the evidence. Her brother   329
couldn't have done it—he had never stolen anything before. Yet   340
here was the proof. What other conclusion was there? Her   350
brother was certainly the criminal.   355

Marie hurried from the cave to look for her brother, eager to   367
know what he would say. But before Marie could find him, one   379
of the Mounties found her. The two met on the trail not far   392
from the cave.   395

The Mountie asked a quick question: "Young woman, can   404
you tell me where I can find Paul Lebrun?"   413

"Paul is my brother," Marie answered.   419

"Then you'll know where he is."   425

"No," Marie said firmly. "I don't know." She gestured toward   435
the horizon. "He has gone away."   441

"Away—where?"   443

"I don't know."   446

For a long quiet moment the Mountie looked at Marie. Then   457
he spoke. "You are lying to me. Why?"   465

"I'm not lying." Marie half shouted. "If you want to know the   477
truth, *I* did it."   481

"Did what?"   483

"Stole the Hudson's Bay furs."   488

"Then you'll know where they are hidden," the Mountie   497
replied.   498

"Of course I do."   502

"Then take me to them."   507

Marie nodded and they started out.   513

As they approached the cave, Marie saw that someone had   523
arrived before them. As they drew closer, she saw that it was   535
her brother. Marie shouted his name to give him an opportunity   546
to escape. But to Marie's astonishment, her brother did not run   557
away but hurried to meet them instead.   564

Marie was equally surprised when the Mountie smiled and   573
extended a friendly hand to Paul.   579

"I think your sister has something to say to both of us," the   592
Mountie said.   594

"I—I have nothing to say," she replied, very confused.   604

"Then let me say it," said the Mountie. "Your brother found   615
Carcajou André with the stolen furs. He took the furs from him   627
and carried them to this cave for safekeeping, and then he   638
came to the police post to tell us about it. We have Carcajou   651
in prison—and now we have the furs. *Now* do you have   663
anything to say?"   666

Marie signified no with a shake of her head.   675

"You have a very loyal sister, Lebrun," said the Mountie.   685

Paul put his arm around Marie.   691

"Oh Paul, I'm so sorry. I thought—" she stammered.   700

"Never mind," said Paul. "Let's go home now. Your feet   710
are wet."   712

Paul Bunyan

by Neil Post

Paul Bunyan was a legendary hero of lumberjacks in the American Northwest. In the late 1800s, logging was one of the hardest and most dangerous jobs in America. Some trees had grown hundreds of feet tall. The fallen branches and rotting stumps on the forest floor were piled higher than the tallest man.

Logging

Loggers would travel up rivers deep into these forests. They'd make a camp and live there for months. It took two men pulling on either end of a long saw to cut down the big trees. Oxen pulled the fallen logs out of woods that were buggy and damp. Huge, slippery rafts of logs many miles long were floated down the rivers to sawmills.

Tall Tales

At night, around the smoky campfires and stoves, men entertained themselves with storytelling. The legend arose of a super logger who could do more things in a bigger way than any other man. Stories of Paul Bunyan first circulated in logging camps in Michigan, Wisconsin, and Minnesota in the Upper Midwest.

15
25
35
45
56
58
59
68
81
95
107
118
123
125
134
143
155
165
174
176

Paul was said to have invented logging and was so big that 188
he could chop down a few miles of trees in a morning. His 201
helper, Babe the Blue Ox, was so big that Paul dug out the 214
Great Lakes as drinking bowls for her. When he and Babe made 226
the Mississippi River, the piles of dirt from the ditch became 237
the Rocky Mountains and the Alleghenies. The 10,000 lakes in 247
Minnesota formed in Babe and Paul's footprints. 254

As the stories spread, they became funny. They were 263
popular even though everyone knew they couldn't really have 272
happened. It was said that Paul Bunyan was so fast he could 284
blow out the lantern and jump back in bed before it was dark. 297
He was also said to have blown the dinner horn so loud that the 311
loggers could ride out of the forest on the echo. Lucy, Paul's 323
purple cow, ate only green grass, so he put green glasses on her 336
in the winter to make the snow look like grass. He once cut 349
down a tree so tall it took three days to fall. 360

Camp life was a large part of Bunyan humor. Paul loved 371
pancakes so much he had a frying pan 235 feet across. Men 383
strapped sides of bacon to their shoes and skated across the 394
hot iron to grease it. The eating tables were so long that the 407
young boys who carried the food down to the end were 418
grandfathers by the time they got back. 425

The Legend Lives On 429

Today, huge machines do the work of Babe the Blue Ox and 441
the mighty Paul Bunyan. Their legend, however, lives on. 450

The Strange Pot

a folktale from China

retold by Julia Perry

3

7

11

20

31

42

54

57

69

78

87

101

113

125

132

141

153

162

164

176

182

191

205

218

225

236

245

256

267

276

Late one afternoon, an old woodcutter was trudging home through the forest. He had worked hard and was very tired. Before long, he spied something shiny behind a big tree stump. It was a huge, old brass pot—the biggest pot the woodcutter had ever seen.

"This would be a fine pot for my wife," he thought. "But how can I carry something so big and heavy?"

The woodcutter thought and thought. Finally, he had an idea. First, he dropped his ax into the pot. Then he tied one end of his rope through the pot's handles and the other end around his body. Pulling and tugging with all his strength, he was able to drag the pot to his cottage.

"What a wonderful pot!" his wife exclaimed happily. "This must have been your lucky day. And you found another ax too."

The woodcutter looked surprised. "Oh no. I only have one ax."

"But there are two axes in the pot," his wife said. "Where did you find the other one?"

Puzzled, the woodcutter peered into the pot. Sure enough, there was a second ax just like the one he had carried. As he reached down to take it out, his cap fell into the pot. Right before his eyes one cap became two!

The old couple became very excited. The old brass pot must possess unusual powers! But how could they test it?

"I have our poor supper prepared," said the wife. "Let's put our meal into the pot and see what happens to it."

When they did the simple meal doubled in size.

56 UNIT 2 • Lesson 7

Intervention

With this, they realized that the pot could make them rich. 287
The old couple had a few coins stored in a cloth bag. They 300
eagerly emptied the coins into the pot and watched as the 311
number of coins doubled. Again and again, they put the new 322
batch of coins into the pot. Before long, every box, bag, bowl, 334
and basket—every pot, pan, plate, and pocket—was filled 344
with coins. 346

"We're rich!" cried the woodcutter. "Now we can build a big 357
house and plant a fine garden." He picked up his wife and 369
twirled her around and around. But in his excitement he 379
accidentally dropped his wife into the pot! 386

"Oh my," said the woodcutter as two women who looked 396
exactly alike climbed from the pot. "How can I have two wives 408
at the same time?" 412

"You can't!" said the first wife. 418

"You can't!" said the second wife. 424

The two wives put their heads together and came up with 435
an idea. They each grabbed one of the woodcutter's arms and 446
tossed him into the pot. 451

Two woodcutters climbed out of the pot. They looked at 461
one another. Then they looked at the two wives. "Oh no! Now 473
there are four of us in one house!" they cried. 483

Fortunately, the clever wives had the answer. They were so 493
rich that each couple was able to construct a big house and 505
plant a fine garden. 509

But from that time on, they were very careful about what 520
went into the pot! 524

The Scoop on Band-Aids
by Grace Drummond

Dirty and Dangerous

"Wash your hands. Don't spread germs." How often have you heard these words? Today we know just how important it is to have clean hands. Keeping your hands clean helps you stay healthy. It also helps stop the spread of germs to others.

Now imagine living in the 1800s. You would never hear the words "Wash your hands. Don't spread germs." At that time, people didn't know about germs and dirty hands.

Imagine what it was like to have an operation in the 1800s. In the 1800s, doctors didn't wash their hands. They didn't wear gloves. And they wore street clothes when they operated. Men stood at the table to look. Do you know what doctors used when they needed bandages? They used pads made from sawdust. It's no surprise that 90% of the patients died in the operating room!

At Last, Clean Bandages

By the 1850s, some doctors saw the connection between germs and disease. They understood how important it was to keep things clean. In the 1850s, two brothers named Johnson started a company. They called it Johnson & Johnson. They made clean bandages from cotton and gauze. Then they sealed the bandages in germ-free packing. Soon they were able to ship the bandages to hospitals and doctors around the country.

In 1920, there was another big change in bandages. At the time, the president of Johnson & Johnson was James Johnson. He heard about a small homemade bandage made by a worker at the company. His name was Earle Dickson. Dickson's wife liked to cook. But she also had lots of little accidents while she cooked. Her cuts and scrapes were too small for a large bandage. So Dickson made a bandage from a small piece of cotton. He used a sticky strip to keep the cotton from getting loose.

10
19
30
41
53
64
74
82
94
105
115
127
136
148
150
154
163
173
183
193
203
214
223
233
243
252
263
275
285
297
310
313

Band-Aids Are Small Bandages   317

But Dickson got tired of making a new bandage every time   328
his wife needed one. So he started making lots of bandages   339
ahead of time. James Johnson watched Dickson make the small   349
bandages. Right away he saw he had a new product. He called   361
it a Band-Aid. At first, the Band-Aids did not sell well. People   373
needed to learn about the product. So the company gave free   384
Band-Aids to Boy Scout troops and butchers. The small   393
bandages became more and more popular.   399

By 1924, Band-Aids were made by machine. Then sales   408
took off. Earle Dickson became a vice-president of the   417
company. It is 80 years since he invented Band-Aids. In that   428
time, more than 100 billion people around the world have worn   439
Band-Aids.   440

Keeping Cool

by G. G. Cohen

The day is hot. Beads of sweat cover your face. Your mouth 18
feels dry. The only thing you can think about is a tall glass of 32
ice-cold water. Well, you are not alone. People have been 42
thinking like this for ages. And they have been doing something 53
about it. 55

Some ancient people cooled their drinks with ice or snow. 65
The Greeks thought that ice cooled the body and made it more 77
active. Without ice, they thought, a person became lazy. Rich 87
Romans spent a lot of time and money to have ice during their 100
hot summers. Slaves were sent up into the mountains. There 110
they packed ice and snow into straw-covered wagons. Then 119
they hauled the wagons back to their masters. 127

In Egypt there are few mountains and the air is always hot. 139
So there is almost no snow or ice. But the ancient Egyptians 151
had other ways to cool drinks. First, they boiled water. Then 162
they left it all night in clay vases to cool. In the morning they 176
wet the outsides of the vases. They placed the vases in deep 189
pits lined with reeds. The reeds and clay kept the heat away 200
from the water. This allowed the Egyptians to have cool drinks 211
for many days. 214

In some parts of the world there is more than enough ice in 227
the winter. The problem in the past was how to save this ice 240
through the summer. 243

In the early United States, George Washington used to have 253
"ice harvests." Washington would cut blocks of ice from the 263
ponds near his home at Mount Vernon. Then he stored it in his 276
icehouses. It stayed as ice for months. 283

By about 1850 many people in the United States were 293
collecting ice. It was needed not only for cooling drinks but for 305
keeping things from spoiling. Butchers, fisherman, and farmers 313
needed ice. It kept their goods fresh before being shipped to 324
market and while on the way there, too. 332

Much of the ice came from parts of the Hudson River. Some 344
also came from the clear lakes of the Northeast and of Canada. 356

As soon as the ice in these areas reached a certain 367
thickness, it was cut into blocks. A horse pulling a cutter (that 379
is, a bar with sharp steel wheels) was driven across the frozen 391
part of the water. The wheels cut back and forth until large 403
blocks had been carved out. 408

Next workers with axes cut the blocks loose. Finally, the 418
blocks were floated to the icehouses on the shore. 427

The first icehouses in the United States were made of wood. 438
This was fine when the ice was taken away in horse-drawn 449
wagons. But then railway lines were built to haul the ice. The 461
wooden houses became dangerous and had to be replaced. The 471
icehouse owners feared that sparks from the train engines 480
would set the wood on fire. So brick houses were built. They 492
cost more, but they were safe. 498

The brick buildings had double walls and thick roofs. 507
Workers stacked ice blocks in the houses. They left space 517
between the blocks. This kept the blocks from melting 526
together. The ice stayed in the houses until it was needed. It 538
could be held there even in the summer. 546

Much of this ice was shipped to tropical countries. First it 557
was moved by train to port cities. There it was loaded onto 569
ships and packed into tin boxes covered with sheepskins. 578
Weeks later, the ship would dock. Then people would enjoy the 589
relief of a cold drink on a hot day. 598

The Polio Doctor

by Molly Reed

Sometimes one doctor has the power to change the lives of millions of people. Such is the case with Dr. Jonas Salk. Through his research, a crippling disease called polio was brought under control around the world.

His Early Medical Work

In medical school, Salk did research in a laboratory. At first, he worked with another doctor to develop ways to prevent the flu. Later his interests turned to polio.

In the 1940s, polio was known to be caused by viruses, which are the smallest germs. Doctors had been studying polio since the 1800s, but they had been unable to slow it down or control it.

Salk searched for a way to somehow weaken the polio virus without harming the human body. In 1953, he announced that he had discovered a possible vaccine. A vaccine is a mixture created to prevent a particular disease.

17
28
37
43
47
58
69
76
87
97
110
112
123
133
144
150

Testing the New Medicine

To show faith in his discovery, Salk took the vaccine first with his wife and three sons. It seemed to be safe and effective. Now it was time to retest it on a much larger scale.

In 1954, Salk's polio vaccine was tested on 1,830,000 American schoolchildren. The results were the same as with Salk's own family. In 1955, the government pronounced his polio vaccine safe and effective.

Recognition for His Greatness

Jonas Salk received many honors for his great achievement. President Eisenhower gave him a special award, and Congress gave him a gold medal for his important work in the field of medicine.

Salk was proud that his vaccine had worked. But he refused to accept any cash prizes for his great discovery.

Today, polio still attacks some adults and children. But thanks to Dr. Jonas Salk, far fewer people are stricken with the disease.

The Shepherd Girl and the Frog

a folktale from Peru

retold by Jeremy Nelson

6

10

14

Once there lived a kind little frog who believed she was ugly. She lived with her brothers and sisters in a sparkling cold stream.

High above the stream, on the side of a mountain, lived a condor. He was the king of birds. The condor's servant was a little shepherd girl he had stolen while she was tending her flock of llamas. Her name was Collyur, meaning "Morning Star." Collyur was sad. She missed her family and wanted to go home very badly.

One morning, Collyur asked the condor, "May I please go to the stream to wash my clothes?"

"No!" growled the condor. "Fix me something to eat."

"Your food is on the table, sir. And my clothes are very dirty."

The condor didn't trust Collyur. He thought she would try to escape.

"I won't, sir, I promise. I must pound my clothes on the rocks to get them clean. You will hear me and know I haven't run away."

"Oh, all right," grumbled the condor.

25

36

38

50

62

73

83

95

97

108

114

123

134

136

146

148

160

173

175

181

Collyur carried her armful of clothes to the stream. She wet   192
the clothes, then began to pound them on the rocks. She was so   205
unhappy that she began to cry.   211

The little frog had watched Collyur for a long time. She felt   223
sorry for the girl. "Dear child, please don't cry. I will help you   236
get home."   238

Collyur was startled at the voice. Then she spied the   248
little frog on a rock. She didn't think the frog was ugly. She   261
saw that it had very kind eyes. Its croaky little voice made her   274
feel better.   276

"Oh, little frog. If only you could."   283

"But I can, sweet Collyur. I have a special kind of power. I   296
can make myself look like anyone I wish to help. To fool the   309
condor, I will look like you and pound your clothes on the rock.   322
You run quickly to the good people who live on the other side   335
of the stream. They will help you to get home."   345

"Oh, thank you, little frog," said Collyur. She gently lifted   355
the frog and kissed its forehead.   361

Then the little frog made herself look just like Collyur. The   372
real Collyur ran across the stream and through the woods.   382
All the while, she could hear the pounding of the clothes on   394
the rocks.   396

Meanwhile, the condor was getting more and more angry.   405
"What is that naughty child doing?" he complained. "All that   415
pounding is giving me a headache. I will go and scold her."   427

But when he flew to the stream, he saw the child walk into   440
the water and vanish! Once again, she was a frog.   450

Back at home, the little frog's brothers and sisters stared   460
at her.   462

"What's the matter?" she asked. "Why are you staring?"   471

"Oh, little sister," they cried, "you have a lovely jewel on   482
your forehead!"   484

Sure enough, right where Collyur had kissed the frog, a   494
beautiful star-shaped jewel sparkled. The jewel looked just like   503
the morning star! And from that day on, the little frog knew she   516
wasn't ugly.   518

The No-Name Disease

by Joanne Baldwin

Magazines make Kara sneeze. Some tissues get her nose running. Takeout Chinese food would make my daughter Kara swell up like a frog.

The postman can't bring a thing to our house. I go down to the post office and get it. I have to go get everything because we just never know what is going to irritate Kara. Kara has a disease. Kara is very sensitive to anything new. Only doctors do not have a name for her illness. They did not even believe us at first. They thought Kara was a hypochondriac, or a person who believes they are sick when they are not.

My Kara is 15 now, but she began getting sick when she was ten. She ate a tuna casserole my aunt sent over for her birthday in August. Her heart started racing. Then her skin became red. We thought it was food poisoning. Another time her tongue became swollen when she ate a frozen pizza. Soon, there was almost nothing she could eat, and Kara began to lose weight.

This went on for about a year. There were only a few things Kara could eat. She ate plain bread I made. She also liked raw vegetables and fruit as long as they weren't sprayed with any chemicals to keep the bugs off. And she could eat steak, too. But only from my neighbor's ranch. Dave Dodge raises his own cattle and doesn't use chemicals.

16
25
30
43
56
69
80
94
105
113
126
139
150
160
171
182
195
208
219
231
242
247

Kara and I got on the Internet and wrote letters. We found   259
seven people in America with the same problem. It seems they,   270
too, are supersensitive to anything new. And their doctors also 280
told them there was nothing wrong with them. So now we've   291
formed a club. We share with each other ways to stay healthy.   303
It's difficult, but it's all we've got.   310

Kara and I live up in a little house behind our main house.   323
My husband and Kara's brothers live down in the main house.   334
They visit twice a week. But they have to shower and wear   346
special clothes that Kara is used to. Plastic sheets are drawn   357
tight over all the windows and doors.   364

Kara has taught me a lot. I eat better foods, and I'm much   377
healthier, too. Maybe this disease does have a name: Karaitis.   387
She's my sweet, cheerful daughter who is healthy now because   397
she takes care of herself.   402

The Goose That Laid the Golden Eggs

adapted from a fable by Aesop

4
7
13

One day a poor farmer and his wife took a basket of apples 26
to market. But no one bought them. When it was time to go 39
home, the basket was still full. 45

But then another farmer came by. He had a skinny old 56
goose under his arm. 60

"I've been unlucky," he said. "I came with a bag of beans to 73
sell. But all I could get for them was this goose. She isn't even 87
worth cooking." 89

"How would you like some apples?" the farmer said. "I'll 99
trade them for that goose. I don't want to carry them home." 111

So they traded. The farmer and his wife took the goose. 122
They went home and put her in the barn. 131

The next morning the farmer went to the barn. The 141
goose had made a nest. When he looked in it, he saw a 154
marvelous thing. 156

Lying in the nest was a golden egg. It was large and shiny. 169
The farmer picked it up. It was very heavy. 178

He ran back to the house. "The most wonderful thing has 189
happened!" he shouted to his wife. "Our goose has laid a 200
beautiful golden egg. It must be worth a fortune." 209

They sold the egg that day. They got more money for it than   222
they had ever seen.   226

The next morning the farmer went back to the barn. There   237
in the nest was another golden egg! Once again they sold the   249
egg for lots of money. They felt rich!   257

The third morning the farmer ran to the barn. Sure enough,   268
there was another golden egg! He took it and went back to   280
the house.   282

"Our goose must have a huge lump of gold inside her," he   294
said to his wife. "Every day she gives us one golden egg. But   307
what if someone should steal her? Then we'd get nothing more.   318
Besides, why should we wait a whole day for one egg? It would   331
be better to kill her now and get all the gold right away."   344

His wife agreed. So with never a word of thanks to the   356
goose for her kindness, they killed the poor creature.   365

They cut her open. To their surprise and dismay, she was   376
just like any other goose inside. There was no gold. All that   388
their greed and impatience brought them was boiled goose   397
for dinner.   399

The point of the story is this: If good fortune comes to you,   412
accept it and be happy. Don't lose what you have by grabbing   424
for more.   426

This fable (a story that teaches a lesson) gave us the   437
expression "to kill the goose that lays the golden eggs." It   448
means being so foolish and greedy that you end up with less   460
than you had before.   464

The Best Doctor in Detroit

by Maya Ferguson

Boyd sat in the waiting room of his sister's office. He   19
enjoyed seeing all the patients who were sitting there with him.   30
He wasn't joyful that people needed a doctor. Since they   40
needed one, though, he was glad they had made the right   51
choice. Boyd's big sister was the best doctor in Detroit!   61

Suddenly, a small lamp in the waiting room made a popping   72
noise and went dark.   76

"The bulb must have burned out," Boyd said. "I'll change it."   87

The boy began to unscrew the old bulb. He forgot how hot   99
it would be.   102

"Ouch!" he said in a loud voice, licking his finger. "How   113
annoying!"   114

"Did you burn yourself?" Ms. Davis asked.   121

"I'm okay," Boyd said. "It only hurts a little at the joint."   133

"Here," Mr. May said, handing Boyd his soda can. "Hold this   144
cold can on the sore spot."   150

Mrs. Cohen snorted, "That's not what you do for a burn. You   162
apply a little butter."   166

"We don't have any butter!" Mr. May laughed.   174

"In my home in China," Ms. Lee said, "my grandmother put   185
soy sauce on burns. I may have some here in my bag."   197

"No, no, no," grunted Mr. Gupta. "In India we use a moist 209
cloth." He moistened a paper towel with water from the sink 220
and handed it to Boyd. 225

"Wrap this around your finger," he said. 232

"No, use ice," Ms. Davis advised. 238

"Better to use butter!" Mrs. Cohen insisted. 245

Just then, Boyd's sister entered the waiting room. She 254
looked around to see who would be next. 262

"Who's next?" she asked with a smile. 269

Everyone pointed to Boyd. He held up his finger for his 280
sister to examine. She immediately took him into her 289
examining room. 291

"A little ointment will do just fine," she said. 300

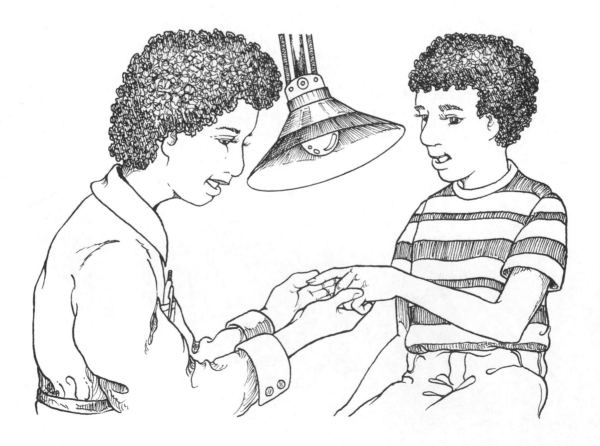

Intervention

A Doctor's Office under Water

by Elizabeth Ann Hamilton

"Next please!"

When you've watched what is going on for a while, you can almost hear those words. The doctor seems to be asking the patient to come into the office. But of course no one says a word. They can't. Both the "doctor" and the "patient" are fish.

A small fish called a wrasse seems to have gone into business. Some wrasses are found in waters round coral reefs. There the sea is full of life. Some of the plants and animals living there are very tiny. In fact, they are so small that they live on the skins of fish. If too many of them grow on a single fish, the fish becomes sick. It may even die.

The wrasse helps keep fish well. It eats the tiny plants and animals growing on the fish. Once again their skins are clean. That makes the fish feel better. And the wrasse has had a free meal.

The wrasse itself is quite small. The fish that come for cleaning are many times its size. Most of these fish like to eat smaller fish. But they never hurt the wrasse. Instead, they remain very still.

The "doctor" nibbles on them with its small, sharp teeth. The wrasse can even swim into their mouths. It will still be safe.

Doctors sometimes wear uniforms. The wrasse has a uniform too. Its body is marked with bright blue and black bars. Most fish are marked so that the other fish can't find them. But the wrasse wants to be seen. It will even swim up to a big fish. It will do a little dance right in front of the fish. It seems to say, "Come to see me if you need help."

5
9
11
23
34
47
58
69
79
92
106
121
129
141
152
164
166
177
190
200
203
213
224
226
234
245
257
271
287
298

Fish don't have to be told about the wrasse. They seem to 310
know that a certain place on the reef is where they'll get help. 323
When their skins start to bother them, they swim to that spot. 335
Sometimes the wrasse is busy. Then they have to wait. If you 347
dived near the reef, you might see many big fish lying in the 360
water. They almost seem to be waiting in line. 369

A diver once saw one small wrasse take care of three 380
hundred fish in six hours. How important this little "doctor" is 391
to the life of a reef. 397

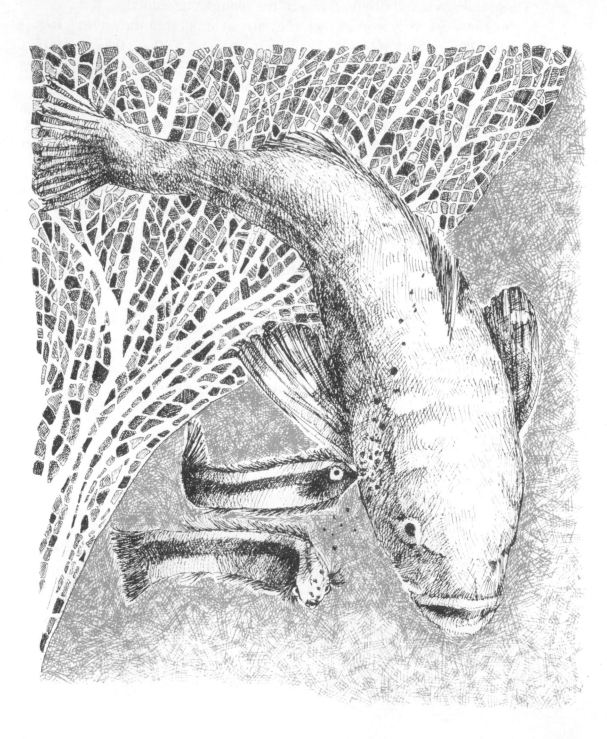

The First Woman Doctor

by Frank Russo

Today there is nothing unusual about seeing a woman
doctor. But in the early 1800s, things were quite different. At
that time, no licensed female doctors were found anywhere in
the United States. People thought only boys should grow up to
be doctors. Girls who wished to study medicine were taught to
be nurses, not doctors.

All that changed with Elizabeth Blackwell, however. She
became the first woman in the United States to receive a
medical degree.

A Determined Student

Elizabeth was born in England in 1821. When she was 11
years old, she and her family moved to New York.

In the 1840s, Elizabeth applied to medical school. She
became a medical student at Geneva College in Geneva, New
York. It was her only choice. Twenty-nine other medical
schools turned her down, simply because she was a woman.

Facing Prejudice

Following her graduation in 1849, Elizabeth traveled to Europe for practical training in hospitals. When she returned to New York, she found herself facing awful prejudice. Few patients came to see her. Hospitals refused to let her enter their rooms. Male doctors avoided and ignored her, too.

Despite these hardships, Elizabeth remained a loyal doctor. In 1857 she and her sister, also a doctor, opened their own hospital. It was called the New York Infirmary for Women and Children. The patients were mostly poor people. Later, Elizabeth opened the Women's Medical College of the New York Infirmary.

Success at Last

Over time, Elizabeth Blackwell managed to gain the respect of both other doctors and her patients. In 1869, she returned to England to continue her work. She wrote several books and lectured a great deal. She helped introduce the idea that cleanliness helps in preventing disease. Dr. Blackwell died in 1910.

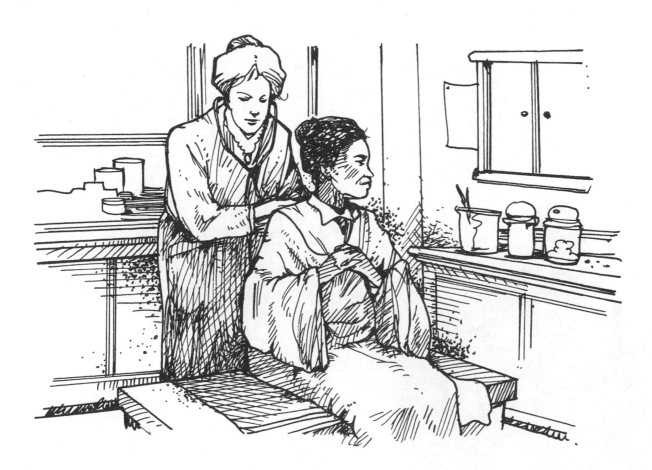

Intervention

The Mystery of the Secret Garden

based on *The Secret Garden* by Frances Hodgson Burnett

The Secret Garden, by Frances Hodgson Burnett, is a book for and about children. It was written more than seventy years ago. But children still love to read it. It tells the story of Mary Lennox.

Mary's parents died when she was only nine. Then she went to live with her uncle, Mr. Craven. His huge house had a hundred rooms.

Mary rarely saw her uncle. His servants took care of her. But there was little for her to do. So she roamed the house and its gardens. She spent most of each day alone.

One of the servants told Mary about a secret garden near the house. It was enclosed in walls. Its door was locked. Ten years before, Mrs. Craven had died after she had a bad fall there. Filled with sadness, Mr. Craven had ordered the garden locked. No one was ever to enter it again; no one was ever to mention it. By the time Mary came, no one even knew where the door and its key were.

How Mary longed to find that garden! She was sure it must be a very wonderful place.

One day Mary found a rusty key buried in the ground. Then   216
a few days later, she discovered the door to the secret garden.   228
It had been hidden by a mass of vines. The key fit the lock.   242
With trembling hands, Mary opened the door.   249

It was the sweetest, most mysterious-looking place anyone   257
could imagine. Here and there climbing vines had crept   266
from one tree to another. They had made lovely bridges of   277
themselves. There were neither leaves nor flowers on them   286
now. Mary did not know whether they were dead or alive.   297
But their hazy tangle from tree to tree made it all look so   310
mysterious.   311

"How still it is!" Mary whispered. "How still!"   319

She waited a moment. She listened to the stillness. A   329
robin, who had flown to his tree top, was still as all the rest.   343
He did not even flutter his wings. He sat without stirring,   354
and looked at Mary.   358

"No wonder it is still," she whispered again. "I am the   368
first person who has spoken here for ten years."   377

With the help of a farm boy named Dickon, who lived   388
nearby, Mary made the garden bloom again. And she learned   398
another secret. Mr. Craven had a son, named Colin. Colin was   409
ill most of the time. He spent his days, grumpy and alone, in   422
bed. He could not walk. No one thought he would live long.   434

One night, Mary found Colin's room. She explained to him   444
who she was. Later, she told him about the garden. Then she   456
and Dickon secretly took him there in his wheelchair.   465

Colin had not been outdoors for years. He had forgotten the   476
smell of spring air. In the garden, he became stronger. He stood   488
up. He walked a few steps!   494

What happened when Mr. Craven learned that the   502
children had gone into the garden? If you read the book,   513
you'll find out. And you'll see why so many people love   524
The Secret Garden.   527

The Barber of Flintville

by Andrew Hill

4

7

Johnny MacEnroe was the best barber in the Wisconsin   16
Territory. That's what he told everybody, anyway. He had   25
learned to cut hair from his aunt. He also had some schooling 37
from a teacher who sent him books in the mail.   47

In 1840, Flintville was a new settlement in the Fox River   58
Valley. A new town needed a blacksmith, miller, merchants, and 68
a barber. Johnny MacEnroe was Flintville's barber. Johnny   76
knew the latest hairstyles. For a nickel, he'd clip a man's nails, 88
wax his moustache, and cut his hair.   95

Johnny's shop became the most popular place in town. Men   105
gathered there not only to get their hair cut but also to talk 118
with each other. Men sat around talking about the news and the 130
weather. History, though, was Johnny's favorite topic.   137

"Did you know that the earliest barbers were doctors, too?"   147
he'd tell his customers. "That's why barbers have a pole out in 159
front of their stores. Those red and white candy stripes look 170
like a bandage. But King Henry VIII of England said only   181
doctors could treat sick people. Barbers were only allowed   190
to cut hair." Then he'd laugh. "But doctors weren't allowed to 201
cut hair!"   203

One day Dave Ferris came in with the worst toothache he   214
had ever had. He begged Johnny to pull his tooth out. Johnny   224
only knew how to cut hair. There was a traveling doctor who   238
came through town once a month. He was off visiting other   249
towns the rest of the time.   255

"Doc Harrison is due here in two weeks," he told Dave. "He 267
can help your tooth. Hang on until then." 275

"The pain is something terrible," Dave begged. "I'll give you 285
a dollar. A real silver dollar!" 291

"I'm not a doctor, Dave," answered Johnny. "I wouldn't 300
know what to do." 304

"You told us that barbers used to pull teeth. You're a barber. 316
Why can't you pull my tooth? I'll give you two silver dollars!" 328

"I can't, Dave," Johnny replied. It wasn't the money. Johnny 338
was scared. He had read a book about pulling teeth, but he 350
wasn't a doctor. Dave was in such pain, but Johnny didn't feel 362
comfortable pulling his tooth. Luckily, the doctor arrived in 371
town a few days early and took care of Dave's tooth. 382

A few weeks after the doctor pulled Dave's tooth, Johnny 392
read about the world's first dental school in Baltimore. Many 402
people in Flintville had problems with their teeth. Flintville 411
needed a dentist. That's when Johnny decided to become a 421
dentist. He went to Baltimore to study dentistry. When he came 432
back, he was the best dentist in the Fox River Valley, and he 445
could cut hair, too. 449

A Royal Confusion

retold from *The Prince and the Pauper* by Mark Twain

*I will tell you an old tale as it was passed down through
the years from father to son. It may be history; it may be only
a legend. It may have happened; it may not have happened;
but it* could *have happened.*

With these words, Mark Twain begins *The Prince and the
Pauper*. This book tells of two boys, born on the same day in
the sixteenth century, in the ancient city of London. One boy,
Tom Canty, was born, unwanted, to a poor family. The other
boy was Edward, Prince of Wales. His birth was cheered by all
of England. The only son of King Henry VIII, Edward would
one day be king.

The boys grew up in the same city. Yet their lives were
worlds apart. Edward lived in a palace, dressed in silks and
velvets. He was loved and cherished by all. Tom, clothed in
rags, lived in dirty, crowded Offal Court. His father beat him
and forced him to beg in the streets. Still, Tom was a bright,
cheerful boy. A kind priest had taught him to read, and Tom
loved reading about royalty. He yearned to meet a real,
live prince.

One day, Tom walked from Offal Court to Westminster. He   220
stared through the palace gates. There, wearing silken clothes   229
that shone with jewels, was a young boy—a prince!   239

Gazing with respect and wonder, Tom leaned up against the   249
gate. A palace guard grabbed him and threw him back into the   261
crowd of onlookers. They pointed and laughed. But the prince   271
leaped to the gate and cried, "How dare you treat a poor lad   284
like that! Open the gates! Let him in!"   292

The prince led Tom into the palace and fed him a grand   304
meal. He listened intently to Tom's tales of life on London's   215
streets. When Tom said that he often dreamed of being a   326
prince, the boys decided to exchange clothes. They stared into   336
the mirror, amazed. They were identical! Without thinking, they   345
agreed to change places secretly for a short time.   354

The boys weren't prepared for what followed. The prince,   363
dressed in ragged clothes, was cast out of the palace gate. Tom,   375
wearing the prince's royal silks, tried to explain the mistake.   385
Everyone, including the king, thought the prince (Tom) was out   395
of his head. Then the king died, and Tom learned that he would   408
soon be crowned the new king—out of his head or not!   420

Meanwhile, Tom's father dragged Edward home to Offal   428
Court, ignoring his claim that he was the prince. The father   439
thought his son had lost his senses. In time, Edward found his   451
way back to the palace and the throne. But his journey was   463
marked with many adventures.   467

Tom, on the other hand, grew comfortable with his role as   478
prince. He even began to act with the dignity and nobility of a   491
true prince. Mark Twain must have believed in the saying   501
"Clothes make the man." When Tom dressed as a pauper, he   512
acted as one and was treated as one. When he dressed as a   525
prince, he behaved and was treated like royalty.   532

Why Do We Have Tears? 5

by Allen Hunter 8

Think about times when you've cried. At first you felt 18
unhappy. Maybe your mouth drooped. Then your eyes 26
scrunched up and got watery. Soon tears were rolling down 36
your cheeks. 38

And sometimes tears drop from your eyes when you are 48
happy. If you laugh very, very hard, tears may spill down your 60
face. But tears have a more important job than showing how 71
you feel. 73

All day long your eyes sit in a bath of tears. These tears 86
keep your eyes clean and healthy. They wash away dirt and 97
germs and other things that get in your eyes. For instance, your 109
eyes water when smoke gets in them. That's because smoke is 120
made of things that bother your eyes. Extra tears come to wash 132
the smoke away. 135

Your eyes also need tears to keep them wet. Your eyes must 147
be wet so that they can move smoothly. All day long, your eyes 160
are busy looking here and there. They move quickly from one 171
thing to another. Right now as you're reading, your eyes are 182
moving along to each word. If your eyes didn't move, you'd 193
have to turn your head to look at things that weren't right in 206
front of you! If you didn't have tears, your eyes couldn't move. 218
And soon you would be blind. 224

But where do all these tears come from? 232

Under each eyelid are tiny sacs called tear glands. That's 242
where tears are made. Every time you blink your eyes, some 253
tears are pushed out of these glands. The tears wash over your 265
eyes and soothe them. 269

When you're not laughing or crying your tears away, where 279
do they go? Tears leave your eyes the way water leaves a sink. 292
The tears go away through small holes in your lower eyelid. 303
These holes are called tear ducts. Some of these holes lead into 315
your nose. Many times when you cry, the tears drip down 326
through your nose—and it starts to run. The drops that fall 338
from your nose are your tears. 344

Maybe you don't like baths, but your eyes can't do without 355
them. All day long, tears wash your eyes to keep them bright 367
and healthy. 369

Hic!

by George R. Paterson

	1
	5

You never know when they'll start. You're reading. Or maybe you're playing. You're minding your own business. All of a sudden you go *hic!* A few seconds pass. You go *hic* again.

"Oh-oh! It's the hiccups. I hope they—*hic*—go away soon!"

The hiccups aren't an illness. They're just something that happens. One of the muscles that helps you breathe starts jerking for no good reason. (Parts of your body do that sometimes.) And that's when you *hic*. The hiccups are as unwelcome as a bad cold. They're a big bother. At first, they may seem funny. You may be sitting in class. You keep going *hic, hic, hic.* Your friends may start to giggle. *Hic, hic, hic!* What if it doesn't stop? Then it's not so funny. If they go on too long, hiccups can make you feel bad. They can make you feel as bad as any illness. They can hurt!

14
24
37
49
58
68
79
89
101
113
125
140
152
160

Most people think they know how to stop hiccups. Just ask   171
them. They'll tell you to hold your breath. Or they may tell you   184
to breathe into a paper bag for a few minutes. Or drink a whole   198
glass of water while you hold your breath. Or drink water from   210
the far side of a glass. (That's hard!) Or get someone to scare   223
you by making a loud noise. Some of these cures seem to work.   236
You might as well try them.   242

One of them might help you. Doctors can't do much for the   254
hiccups. There are a few medicines that help to stop the   265
hiccups sometimes. But most doctors just tell you to wait. Wait   276
till the hiccups go away. And that's fairly good advice, because   287
most of the time they last only a short while.   297

But Charles Osborne wasn't so lucky. He hiccupped every 306
one and a half seconds for sixty-nine years and five months— 318
from the autumn of 1922 to February of 1990—before his 329
hiccups went away. That's 1,460,000,000 times—or one billion 338
four hundred sixty million *hics!* 343

What finally cured him? No one knows. Maybe he scared 353
himself with an extra loud *HIC!* 359

Surviving the Storm

by Lauren Friedland

Eric was surprised by what he just read on his watch. "I can't believe it is only 2:00 P.M.!" said Eric to Kate. It was dark in the woods. Suddenly, there was a bolt of lightning and thunder. Jessie, the camp group guide, spoke as loud as he could.

"We must get away from the trees and into an open field as quickly as we can," Jessie said. "Hold your buddy's hand. I will whistle every so often. After you hear me whistle, count off. If you get lost, stay where you are, listen for the whistle, and shout your name. I will help you."

There was lightning and thunder all around. It was raining hard. Kate and Eric stood holding hands watching the lightning in the sky. It was awesome. Just then, Eric tripped. Kate stopped to see if he was hurt.

"What do we do now?" Eric asked Kate in a trembling voice after he had gotten up. The two children could no longer hear the footsteps and voices of the rest of the group.

"We can't move very fast and we can't see where we are   195
going," Kate said. "Let's wait here. After we hear Jessie's   205
whistle, we can shout our names for help." Eric and Kate saw   217
more lightning. They squatted close to the ground on their   227
backpacks and waited for Jessie's call.   233

As soon as the group got to an open field, Jessie asked   245
everyone to squat on their backpacks. Then, Jessie whistled.   254
But before the count-off started, everyone heard Eric and Kate   264
shout their names. Jessie told everyone to wait in the field. He   276
was going back to get Eric and Kate.   284

Jessie ran back into the woods and shouted, "Eric! Kate!"   294
over and over again. Each time Eric and Kate listened to   305
the loudness of Jessie's voice and footsteps to see if he was   317
getting closer. They shouted back to Jessie either "Closer!"   326
or "Farther!"   328

Finally, Jessie was standing in front of them. Together, they   338
made it to the field safely and joined the others.   348

Meet the Koala

by Kit Murphy

3
6

Imagine you are visiting a friend in Australia. You go for a hike in the forest. Suddenly, your friend shouts, "Look up!"

There's a furry, gray animal in a leafy tree. What is it? No, it's not a squirrel. It's not an opossum, either. Can you guess what it is? It's a koala.

The koala looks like a teddy bear. But it's not a bear at all. The koala is a marsupial. A marsupial is a mammal with a pouch. A kangaroo is a marsupial, too. A female marsupial has a pouch on her underside. This is where her babies live after they are born.

A newborn koala is the size of a lima bean. The baby can't protect itself and must crawl into its mother's pouch. Inside the pouch, the baby gets milk. Gradually, it grows larger. After eight months, the baby is ready to come out. It can start eating a koala's favorite food—leaves from the eucalyptus, or gum, tree.

At one time, these trees covered large parts of Australia. Koalas filled the forests. Then, people cut down the trees. It looked as if koalas might disappear.

Now koalas are protected. They live in parks and in the wild. If you ever go to Australia, remember to look up. You might see a koala.

18
28
41
53
59
73
85
96
108
111
124
135
146
159
169
179
190
196
207
219
223

First Step to the Top of the World

by Beth Malone

Peary's Dream

Even as a child, Robert E. Peary had a dream of doing something big. In fact, he had one hope—that he would be the first to do something important.

Peary was a good student. He loved nature and adventure. He once had a dream that he would be the first person to walk on the North Pole. He made this dream his goal and worked toward it for 23 years.

The Dangerous North

His first step was to take a trip to Greenland. He wanted to find answers to questions that were unanswered at that time. Was Greenland an island? Was Greenland connected to land that went to the North Pole? He also wanted to test equipment and tools he would need later.

Peary planned to make the trip alone. But then he met a young man, Christian Maigaard, who was excited about his idea. They decided to make the trip together.

The men found the frozen north filled with more dangers than they imagined. They faced fierce blizzards with heavy snowfall and harsh winds. But the worst dangers were the crevasses—huge, deep cracks in the ice. Some were as wide as 50 feet, and sometimes they were hidden in snow.

13
25
38
43
53
67
79
84
87
100
110
119
131
137
149
158
166
176
185
195
207
216

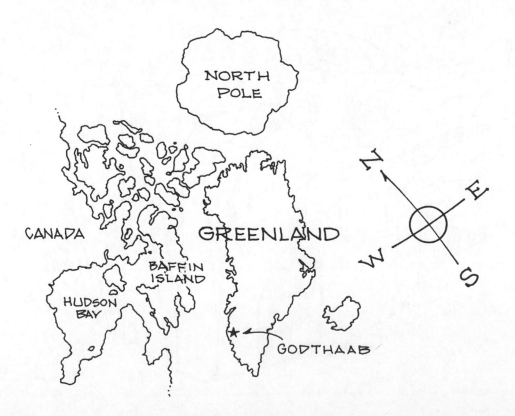

Usually a rope tied Peary and Maigaard together so they 226
wouldn't lose each other. One day they were circling a 236
crevasse, and Maigaard lost his footing. One leg was hanging in 247
a crack in the ice that was hidden by snow. When Peary felt his 261
rope pull, he knew Maigaard was in trouble. Peary hung on to a 274
chunk of ice, hoping it wouldn't break while he was holding it. 286

Maigaard didn't know how deep the crack was, and he 296
didn't know if the rope would hold. Luckily, the rope that was 308
tied to Peary kept him from falling deeper into the crack. 319
Slowly, Maigaard pulled on the rope and tried to move out of 331
the crevasse. He slowly moved through the snow, looking for 341
any rough piece of ice he could pull on. 350

Maigaard found a small bump of ice. He pulled at it, and it 363
held. He slowly pulled himself up. Peary's rope and clear 373
thinking had saved Maigaard from a fall and probably his death. 384

Greenland at Last! 387

In his notes, Peary called Greenland "an Arctic Sahara." It 397
did seem like a desert. There were no animals, plants, rocks, or 409
soil. Instead there was frozen land, white, bright sun, and 419
endless blue sky. 422

Peary and Maigaard traveled about 100 miles from where 431
they started. They accomplished what they set out to do. They 443
had traveled farther across Greenland than anyone else. 450

Vanishing Wildlife

by Sue Salvanius

2

5

The last dodo died around 1681. Since then, at least eighty-five other kinds of birds have disappeared from the face of the earth. So have forty other animals.

Now, in the 1990s, over eight hundred other kinds of animals live threatened lives. They are threatened by men. Sometimes men have had to kill pests that harm crops. Sometimes men have had to kill wild animals in order to protect themselves and their herd animals. Sometimes men have had to cut down forests and clear swamps in order to plant and build. But sometimes men have just been careless. They have caused forest fires. They have poisoned the air and water with wastes. Sometimes men have had no excuse. And now many animals are in danger.

The cheetah is one. Humans have destroyed its home and hunting grounds. They have killed the animal in great numbers. Its fur, like the leopard's, is used for coats.

The ivory-billed woodpecker, the Hawaiian crow, and the imperial woodpecker are three birds that are in trouble. The forests they lived in have been cut down. They have no nesting places. They can't raise their young.

16
28
34
44
53
63
74
82
94
104
115
125
131
141
151
160
168
178
190
196

The woolly spider monkey is another animal that is   205
disappearing. Its forest home is also being cut down. Now it is   217
the rarest New World monkey.   222

There are now only five thousand orangutans in the world.   232
This likable ape has been hunted for zoos and pet shops. The   244
few that are left can live only if the laws that protect them   257
are enforced.   259

The Japanese crane, the giant ibis, and the whooping crane   269
are nearly gone. There are only a few birds of each kind left.   282

Other animals may soon be gone forever. The tamarau is a   293
small water buffalo. It is being killed off by hunters. So is the 306
anoa, a wild ox. The Tasmanian wolf once roamed all of   317
Australia and New Zealand. But nobody has seen one since the   328
1960s. The Sumatran rhinoceros now lives only in small herds   338
on game preserves. One herd has only six animals in it. The   350
giant otter of South America will be gone if hunting and   361
trapping aren't controlled. In Asia, the lion is almost gone.   371
Several kinds of deer, several kinds of bear, and several kinds   382
of seal are here today. But maybe not tomorrow.   391

You may never have heard of some of these animals and   402
birds. You may never see them. If laws are not passed to   414
protect them, you may never have a *chance* to see them. And   426
those laws must be obeyed. It will take a lot of people, all over 440
the world, working together to save the vanishing wildlife. It's 450
probably too late for some. But others could still be saved.   461
Maybe you'll find a way to help.   468

Water Crushes Steel

by Nick Ramirez

My father takes a golf cart to the bow. It's too far to walk. He's the captain of one of the largest oil tankers in the world. She's called the *Petrol Princess*. She's taller than a 15-story building. She's longer than four football fields. It takes five miles just to stop her once she gets going because she is so big.

On my 13th birthday, my birthday present was a ride on the *Petrol Princess*. My mom didn't want me to go. But my dad promised a short run from Baltimore to Quebec. The sea was calm when we left. It was actually very boring, but that didn't last very long.

Unexpected Problems

Then the rudder broke. That's the part that steers the ship. It wouldn't move. We had to turn the engines off. We drifted free while Dad and his men tried to fix the rudder. It's the size of a huge billboard, and they couldn't move it at all.

They told the Coast Guard to keep other ships out of the way. We were far out at sea. There was little chance of hitting any land, so we didn't have anything to worry about. Sooner or later, the men would fix the rudder, and we'd be fine. As long as the weather held, we could drift almost forever without having any major difficulty.

Rough Seas 233

Then a small, rainy storm off to the south hit a cold front. 246
The two became a hurricane. The waves rose from 10 feet to 50 259
in a few hours. The wind started really blowing. The rain hit the 272
windows like bullets. The steel wires that held up the radio 283
antenna started humming. Their sound told my dad the wind 293
was nearly 100 miles an hour. 299

The huge ship rode up the front of each wave like a toy 312
boat. As the wave broke, tons of water smashed down on the 324
deck. Then the *Petrol Princess* would fall down the back of 335
the monster wave. We'd plow into the water. The whole ship 346
would shake. 348

Without a rudder, the wind threw the giant ship around like 359
a stick in a river. Then a rogue wave smashed into us. A rogue 373
wave is one in a thousand. It broke the windows in the control 386
room one hundred and ten feet up. The weight of all that water 399
ripped the steel doors off. The ocean poured into the inside of 411
my father's beautiful ship. 415

Help Arrives 417

She was sinking fast. We put on our life preservers. Then we 429
climbed into lifeboats. The Coast Guard helicopters arrived. 437
The wind blew them around like insects. One by one, they lifted 449
us off the lifeboats by a cable. It was the scariest thing I ever 463
did. My dad was last. Then the *Petrol Princess* disappeared 473
under another big wave. 477

On our way back to land, my dad turned to me. He said that 491
for my 14th birthday, we'd go miniature golfing. 499

He Chose to Succeed

by Ron Travis

"You might say I was lucky. And I was. But I made a choice." 21

Edward James Olmos is speaking to a group of men in a 33
prison. The famous Hispanic-American actor is telling them 41
about his life. He tells them that you don't have to be born rich 55
to have the life you want. He also wants them to know that he 69
cares about them. 72

Edward was born in East Los Angeles. The people living 82
around him came from many different countries. "I thought that 92
was what the world was like," he says. He remembers it as a 105
wonderful place. 107

He came from a large family, but things weren't always easy. 118
When he was eight, his parents separated. Edward began to 128
play baseball. He liked seeing his father at every game. He got 140
so good that he was the state batting champion. 149

Then, he taught himself to play the piano and sing. When he 161
was fourteen, he started playing with a rock band. He admits 172
that he wasn't a very good singer and adds, "But, boy, could I 185
scream and dance!" Edward went to school during the day and 196
played in the band at night. He took acting classes to help with 209
his singing. But he found out that he liked acting more. 220

Edward married and had two sons. He worked at many jobs 231
to support his family. Finally, he got a job acting in a play that 245
ran for over a year. He won two awards for the play. After that, 259
Edward began to get good parts in movies. Then he took a role 272
in the television show *Miami Vice*. 278

Edward believes in making his characters seem as real as 288
possible. When he played a teacher in the movie *Stand and* 299
Deliver, he gained forty pounds. He spent hours getting made 309
up to look like the man he was playing. He almost won an 322
Oscar, an acting award, for that part. 329

Edward often speaks to young people in schools, hospitals, 338
and prisons. He wants them to know that they can become 349
anything they want to be. He tells them about his own life. He 362
says he would make up his mind and stick with it. "Success 374
really bounces you around," he says. Edward says that you 384
have to be true to your beliefs, even after you are famous. 396

When Edward returns to his old neighborhood, it makes 405
him sad. It is still very poor and run-down. He would like to 419
turn the small house where he grew up into a museum. It 431
would "show kids that starting from here, they can go 441
anywhere they want." 444

Edward says that he's not trying to tell people to be like 456
him. But his life is a good model. ". . . I come from a [broken] 469
family," he says. "I'm a minority. I have no natural talent, but 481
I did it. If I can do it, anybody can do it. I take away all the 498
excuses." 499

Grinning the Bark off a Tree

by Joan Burns

6

9

A Real and Made-Up Man

There was a real Colonel David Crockett, and there was a made-up Davy Crockett. They were both the same man. The real David used the made-up Davy to win a seat in Congress. To most of us today, however, the two Crocketts have become confused.

The real David was born in Tennessee in 1786. At that time, there weren't many Americans settled in that area. Native Americans were fighting to keep their land. David's family was one of the first European families to enter Native American land. Life was hard. He lived in a crude cabin and had to hunt in the forest for food. At age 12, David went to work. He drove cattle 400 miles on foot and earned six dollars.

This hard life became part of Davy's story. Later, as a man, he told funny stories about hunting. People passed these stories around. They started to believe that the stories were true. A legend was born. Davy Crockett became the best hunter, woodsman, and tough guy in the wilderness.

14
25
36
50
60
61
73
82
92
102
116
130
139
151
161
172
181
188

The Legend

People said he could catch a bear just by hugging him. He saved bullets by grinning at raccoons so hard they fell out of trees. Legend says that one time he grinned at a raccoon but it wouldn't move. So he chopped the tree down. Then he saw it wasn't a raccoon at all. A big knot in the tree just looked like a raccoon. Davy saw that he had grinned so hard all the bark fell off the tree.

Davy was said to be a perfect shot. His rifle, Betsy, was almost as famous as he was. He could shoot a comb out of a woman's hair.

The Hero

People called him a ring-tailed roarer because he talked so much. They said he was half-crocodile and half-horse. The truth remains, David or Davy was a funny storyteller. He may have had little education, but he was honest and brave. And he used his image as one of the first heroes in our young country to lead men and women.

David Crockett's life became part of American history. He later fought in the Indian Wars of 1813. When he was elected to Congress, he fought for the rights of Native Americans in Washington. He became famous as the "Coonskin Congressman." He wore a hat made from the skins of raccoons. He died fighting at the Alamo in Texas.

Like all heroes, the truth about Davy Crockett is mixed up with the stories. Yet both the made-up Davy and the real David were larger than life.

190
202
214
227
239
254
267
270
282
296
298
300
310
320
331
343
356
360
369
382
392
399
410
418
429
441
445

The Largest Animals in the World   6

The ice-cold water near the South Pole is the summer home   17
of the largest animals that have ever lived—whales. That's right.   28
The blue whale, the giant of the whale family, can grow to be   41
bigger than two dinosaurs. It can be heavier than twelve   51
elephants. One of its eyes might be the size of a small child.   64

Though whales look much like fish, they are not fish.   74
Whales need air. They must hold their breath underwater. If   84
they stay under too long, they will drown. That makes them   95
very different from fish.   99

If the whale is not a fish, then what is it?   110

It is a mammal just as you are. It has hair, though very little   124
of it. It is warm-blooded. Baby whales, called calves, are born   135
live. A baby whale drinks milk from its mother's body. All this is   148
true of people, too. That is how it is that you and a whale are   163
both mammals.   165

Whales are too big to keep in zoos. Most people never see   177
one. If only you could watch them at sea! When whales come   189
up for air, they make quite a noise. They blow out the air they   203
have held in their lungs. It is warm air. When it hits cooler air, it   218
turns to steam. The steam pours out of a hole on top of the   232
whale's head. This is called the whale's *spout*. The steam from a   244
whale's spout can be seen for a long way.   253

The full-grown blue whale gets food in a strange way. Some   264
whales have teeth, but not the blue whale. Instead, it has a kind   277
of curtain that hangs from the roof of its mouth. This curtain is   290
called *baleen*. It is made of fine whalebone. When the whale   301
wants to feed, it opens its mouth wide and swims full speed   312
ahead. Soon its huge mouth is filled with water. In the water   324
are thousands of tiny sea animals and plants. The whale then   335
closes its mouth and pushes the water out with its tongue. The   347
water shoots out through the curtain. But the food stays   357
trapped in the whale's mouth. It takes many mouthfuls to fill up   369
such a big animal.   373

For much of the year whales live in warm seas. That is   385
where their calves are born. But warm waters are not as rich in 398
food as cold waters. So when the calves are strong enough, the   410
whales move south. Blue whales may swim halfway around the   420
world to reach the water near the South Pole. Their smooth   431
skin helps them swim quickly. They rest by taking little naps as 443
they float on top of the water. Finally, they reach the cold sea. 456
And the summer feast begins. The food there will make them   467
fat and will help them live through the coming year.   477

Mount Pelée

by Jill Jacobs

Gaston lived with his father, Philippe, on the island of Martinique. In April 1902, the island's volcano, Mount Pelée, woke up. It had been quiet for as long as anyone could remember. But now it awoke and shook the island with earthquakes. Clouds of ashes spewed from the top and frightened Gaston and his father.

Others thought Mount Pelée was harmless until its ashes started to fall like snowflakes on Saint Pierre, the largest city on the island. Ashes covered the roads and roofs. The horses and carriage wheels made no sound on the stone streets, and the air started to smell like sulfur. After a few days, people started to fear Mount Pelée.

In May, when Philippe heard that poison vapors from the volcano had killed birds and plants on the mountain, he warned Gaston that they needed to leave the island. Some already had left. Philippe and Gaston could not leave because they had no money. Philippe then decided to sell all he had to buy a boat. The father and son hurried to the crowded harbor but found they did not have enough money to buy a boat.

Philippe knew they needed to find a safe place to survive the volcano's fury. He remembered visiting the old castle of Saint Pierre a long time ago.

15
24
36
46
55
60
69
80
91
102
114
119
129
140
151
162
175
186
196
207
217
223

"Surely the castle is safe," he said to his worried son. 234

They ran to the castle gate and called for the guard. To their 247
surprise, no one appeared. When Philippe knocked, the door 256
swung open. 258

"Where is everyone?" Gaston wondered. 263

The two called out, but no one replied. Since it was growing 275
dark, the pair decided to stay the night in the stone castle. In 288
the morning they would explain to the guard. 296

Shortly after dawn, four huge booms like cannon shots 305
awakened them. Looking out the window, they saw Mount 314
Pelée had blown open its side. 320

"Quick!" Philippe yelled. "Run to the bottom of the castle!" 330

They dashed down the staircase to a cold stone room well 341
below the ground's surface. Just then a huge cloud rushed 351
toward the town of Saint Pierre. This boiling-hot cloud of gas 363
and ash rolled like an avalanche over the city, destroying 373
houses and killing thousands. Even ships at sea caught on fire. 384

Gaston and his father survived the volcano's eruption. The 393
thick stone walls and the depth of the castle's basement had 404
protected them from the boiling cloud of gas and ash. Later 415
they learned that this floor once had been part of a jail. It was 429
lucky for Gaston and Philippe that the walls that once had 440
kept prisoners from escaping also prevented outside forces 448
from entering! 450

Whatever Happened to the Dinosaurs?

by Karen Stevens

2
5
8

At on time, dinosaurs ruled the earth. In fact, these huge reptiles roamed the earth freely for more than 150 million years. After so much time, why did the dinosaurs disappear?

That's one of the great mysteries of science. Scientists have debated the question for years. They've come up with a number of theories. Those theories include everything from diseases to floods to attacks by space aliens.

Today, two theories are popular. One theory says that the dinosaurs disappeared because of changes in the earth's geography. The other says that the earth was hit by a giant object that fell from outer space.

First, let's examine the geography theory. Today, the earth has seven continents. But that was not true when dinosaurs lived here. At that time, five continents were grouped together in one supercontinent. By the end of the dinosaur's reign, the supercontinent had broken apart. Its pieces had begun to drift away. Eventually, they became five of the continents we know today.

19
29
39
49
60
69
75
85
93
105
111
120
130
140
150
160
170
172

The movement of the continents, called continental drift,   180
caused many changes. Once, dinosaurs could wander all over   189
the planet. They may have migrated seasonally. For example,   198
they may have moves south to escape harsh winters or to look   210
for food. Then the continents broke apart. The dinosaurs could   220
no longer migrate.   223

The continental drift also changed the earth's climate. The   232
supercontinent had many inland seas. The inland seas warmed   241
the winter air. Winters were mild. When the continents broke   251
apart the seas drained into the ocean. Winters became much   261
colder. Perhaps the dinosaurs could not adapt to the climate   271
changes. Gradually, they died out.   276

Of course, in this case, *gradually* means "*very, very* slowly."   286
The dinosaurs didn't die out overnight. The process of   295
becoming extinct may have taken millions of years. We know   305
that the continental drift itself took a very long time to happen.   317

But perhaps the continental drift did not cause the   326
extinction of the dinosaurs. Another popular theory is called   335
the impact theory. It says that something struck the earth with   346
a tremendous impact, or force. The object that stuck the earth   357
may have been a huge asteroid—one of a small group of   369
planets between Mars and Jupiter. Or it may have been many   380
asteroids, or even a comet.   385

A scientist named Walter Alvarez was the first to develop   395
the impact theory. During the 1970s, Alvarez was working in   405
Italy. Inside some rock, he found a very interesting layer of clay.   417
The clay came from the end of the Cretaceous period, the last   429
period of the dinosaurs.   433

Alvarez shipped the clay home. With a team of researchers,   443
he studied it in a laboratory. The clay, they found, contained a   455
large amount of iridium, a silver-white metal. Iridium is rare on   466
the earth's surface. But it is common in meteors, which come   477
from outer space. Alvarez and his team thought that the iridium   488
they found might also have come from outer space.   497

If so, how did it get into the rock? Perhaps it came from an 511
asteroid that fell from space and hit the earth. The asteroid was 523
huge. When it struck, it created great clouds of dust. Those 534
clouds were bigger than any ever seen by humans. 543

With the help of a computer, the team could see what those 555
clouds may have been like. They figured out that the clouds 566
would have been large enough to block out the sun. The 577
clouds, they believed, stayed in the earth's upper atmosphere 586
for months. 588

How did the dust clouds kill the dinosaurs? They destroyed 598
important parts of the food chain. They blocked the sunlight, 608
which plants need to live. As a result, many plants died. In turn, 621
the animals that fed on the plants died. Plant-eating dinosaurs 631
were among them. 634

Meat-eating dinosaurs were in trouble too. They fed on 643
plant-eating animals. When the plant-eating animals began to 652
die, the meat-eating dinosaurs faced starvation. The dinosaurs 660
were extinct within months. So were many other living things. 670

Many scientists don't accept the impact theory. They don't 679
believe that the dinosaurs could have died out so quickly. 689
Fossils, they say, show that the extinction of the dinosaurs took 700
millions of years. Some of these scientists favor the continental 710
drift theory. 712

But since Alvarez's discovery, others have discovered 719
iridium fossil beds all around the world. Their findings support 729
the impact theory. 732

Which theory is correct? No one knows for sure. Maybe 742
neither theory is correct. Or maybe they both are. The answer 753
to the mystery may lie in a combination of theories. Some 764
scientists think that the dinosaurs were already ailing when the 774
asteroid hit the earth. The asteroid merely finished them off. If 785
this is true, then perhaps the continental drift was what 795
weakened the dinosaurs in the first place. Or maybe it was 806
something else. We may never know. 812

The Hiding Place

by Morgan Reese

3

6

Corrie ten Boom lived in Holland with her father and sister. 17
Her father was a watchmaker. The Dutch family lived in a large 29
house above the watch shop. 34

During World War II, Nazi Germany took control of 43
Holland's cities and towns. Troops rounded up many Jews off 53
the streets. Trains carried them to German factories, labor 62
camps, and concentration camps, where they were forced to 71
work as slaves. Those who couldn't work were killed. 80

A Dangerous Plan 83

Corrie couldn't believe what was happening in her 91
homeland. She wanted to help those Jews who had not yet 102
been captured and taken away. She and her family decided to 113
use their home as a hiding place. 120

Corrie knew the plan was dangerous. Nazis often raided 129
houses, looking for Jews. If found out, the whole ten Boom 140
family might be killed. 144

Corrie met a man who was able to build a secret space in 157
the house. It was behind a fake wall in Corrie's bedroom, on 169
the top floor. The space was big enough to hold six people. 181
Soon, six Jewish guests were staying with the family. 190
Meanwhile, Corrie found other homes in Holland where more 199
Jews could hide. 202

UNIT 4 • Lesson 6

Intervention

A Surprise Raid

205

One day, the Nazis raided the ten Boom home. The 215
guests hid in the secret room before the Nazis could get up 227
the staircase. 229

The Jews were never discovered, but Corrie's entire family 238
was arrested anyway. They went to jail, where Corrie's father 248
died. Later, Corrie and her sister were sent to a labor camp, 260
where her sister died. Only Corrie survived among her family. 270

After the war, word of Corrie's brave deeds spread. She 280
traveled around the world to share her amazing story of 290
survival. She died in 1983, at the age of 91. 300

Wilderness Friends

by Wiley Blevins

Mary's father saddled up the horse as he prepared to leave 16
for Boston. "It'll be okay," he said as he gave Mary a big hug. 30
"Don't stray too far from the cabin. I'll return soon." Every time 42
her father went to Boston to get supplies, Mary was worried he 54
wouldn't come back. It was unsafe to travel through certain 64
parts of the colonies. Also, Mary did not like it when she and 77
her mother had to stay home alone in the wilderness. But her 89
father had gone to Boston before and had always returned 99
safely. And she and her mother had always been safe at home. 111

Because it was late November and there was a chill in the 123
air, Mary wanted to keep a strong fire going all night. Her 135
mother was feeling ill, and a warm cabin would help. 145

Mary had spent hours cutting and gathering wood for the 155
fire. When she returned to the cabin, something was terribly 165
wrong. The pot of stew was boiling rapidly over the fireplace, 176
but her mother was missing. 181

A faint moan from outside the cabin broke the silence, and 192
Mary ran outside. There she found her mother on the ground, 203
holding her stomach. Mary felt her mother's forehead and 212
realized she was burning with fever. 218

"Mary," her mother whispered, "if you help me inside and   228
make me some tea for my fever, I'll be okay."   238

Mary knew that chickweed and feverfew were some of the   248
best plants to use for making medicines and that they were   259
especially good for fevers and upset stomachs. Boiled yellow-   268
eyed daisies also made a good tea that helped cure coughs.   279

"But Mama," cried Mary, "we are all out of chickweed."   289

"Mary," her mother whispered, "you must gather some and   298
make medicine."   300

Mary knew she would have to walk far into the woods to   312
gather the herbs. What if she was attacked?   320

Mary helped her mother into bed and covered her with   330
extra blankets. Then she went in the kitchen and found a   341
basket and a small candle. She knew she had to be brave. She   354
put on her cloak, lit the candle, and walked out into the cool   367
night air.   369

Mary could find no chickweed or feverfew near the cabin,   379
and she knew she would have to go farther.   388

She plodded deeper into the forest. Even though it was   398
getting dark, she could still see the tracks of large animals. The   410
owls were already out searching for their late-night snacks.   419
Every strange noise made her heart pound.   426

Then Mary heard the sounds of sticks cracking underneath   435
footsteps, and she froze in her tracks. Quickly, she hid behind a   447
tree and blew out her candle. If she remained quiet, she would   459
be safe. The footsteps came closer and then stopped.   468

Mary sat awhile, motionless, but she knew she had to find   479
the herbs and return to her mother. Slowly, she stood up and   491
turned around. There, standing in front of her, was someone or   502
something with large, glowing eyes. Mary dropped the basket   511
and raced away with all her might.   518

She could barely see, but the smell of the fire burning in the   531
fireplace helped her retrace her steps home. With one last burst   542
or energy, she ran inside the cabin and locked the door with the   555
wooden latch.   557

"How will I explain that I have returned with no medicine?"   568
she thought as she sat beside her sleeping mother.   577

The next morning, Mary awakened to a noise outside the cabin. "Maybe it's father," she thought as she unlatched the door and peeked outside. In front of the door was the same pair of glowing eyes she had seen the night before. But instead of something fearsome, a girl about Mary's age was standing there in a soiled, tattered dress. "Help me," the girl whispered.   587 597 609 621 631 642

Mary brought her inside the cabin and handed her some bread and stew.   652 655

"Where did you come from? How did you get here? What is your name?" Mary rapidly asked.   667 672

"I'm Sarah, and I'm lost," the girl said as she began to cry. "I was out gathering wood when it got dark. I just kept walking and walking, but I couldn't find my cabin. My family must be very concerned."   686 698 710 712

Mary saw how terrified Sarah looked. "As soon as you finish eating," she assured Sarah, "I'll help you find your home. Besides, I need to go into the woods and find some medicine for my mother."   723 733 745 748

Sarah glanced over and saw that Mary's mother was sweating with fever. "I think I can help," she said. "The bark of the willow tree is perfect medicine for a fever."   757 770 779

Mary grabbed a basket as she and Sarah left the cabin to look for the bark and some chickweed. After a long search, they returned. Sarah lifted Mary's mother's head and held out a piece of bark for her to chew on, while Mary boiled some of the chickweed and made a soothing tea. Mary knew her mother would be fine.   791 802 813 827 837 840

Before nightfall, Mary had helped Sarah find her cabin. Sarah's worried family were so grateful to see her again that they baked special treats for Mary to take back to her mother. Although Sarah lived over three miles away, Mary visited often. Soon the two wilderness friends became *best* friends. Sarah never forgot how Mary had helped her find her cabin, and Mary never forgot how Sarah had helped save her mother's life.   849 860 872 882 891 903 913

What Are the Wolves Saying?

by Susan Ring

You are walking through the snow on a winter day. All is
quiet until you hear howling from far away. What could it be?
You are not quite sure and walk a bit more. Suddenly you come
upon some footprints in the snow. You look in the tracking
book and see that you have come across the footprints
of a wolf.

Wolf Talk

Wolves live in a group called a pack. Most packs have about
eight members. The pack is run by very strong wolves. The
stronger wolves stand tall and point their ears up. They may
also show their teeth or growl. The weaker members of the
group let them know they are the leaders. How do they do this
without words? The lower-ranking pack members hold their
tails between their legs and turn down their ears. They also
may whine.

There are many other ways that wolves talk to each other.
They use different sounds and body language that mean certain
things. Have you ever seen a dog wag its tail when it's happy?
Wolves do that, too. They also use their ears to communicate.
When they get scared, their ears lie flat against their head.
When they show their teeth, they are angry. They warn about
danger by barking. Wolves also howl to communicate with
each other.

Wolves hunt when they are hungry any time of the day or
night. They need to find food just the way lions and bears and
other animals do. They will eat something as small as a mouse
or as big as a deer. Almost any kind of animal will do. When
they hunt a large animal, they hunt in a pack. When the pack
gathers to hunt, they greet each other with a howl. This howl
also warns other wolves to stay away from their territory. Have
you ever heard a wolf howl? One wolf, or two or three, will put
their noses in the air and make a high, singing sound. Before
you know it, other wolves join in and the whole pack is
howling away. It definitely makes a noise, but the noise serves
a real purpose.

20
32
45
56
66
69
71
83
94
105
116
129
137
148
150
161
171
184
195
206
217
226
228
240
253
265
279
292
304
315
329
341
353
364
367

Something to Howl About   371

    There are other reasons why wolves howl. There are many   381
different howls with special meanings for different occasions.   389
Wolves also have different howls for communicating and   397
hunting. If a wolf has lost the rest of his pack, he will howl to   412
let the others know exactly where he is. We have read that   424
wolves howl before hunting. They also may howl after hunting,   434
after eating, and when an intruder is close by. A howl can be   447
heard as far as ten miles away! Sometimes wolves howl just for   459
fun, at any time of the day or night. Some people think wolves   472
howl only at the full moon. This is not true. Wolves always   484
know how to talk to one another. That's why they howl in the   497
first place.   499

Gwendolyn Brooks, Poet

by Tamara Bott

David and Keziah Brooks were happy and surprised when
they saw their daughter Gwendolyn's writing. The poems were
good. They were just two lines each. But they filled a whole
page. And the poet was only seven years old!

Gwendolyn's mother made a prediction. Gwendolyn would
become a famous poet. The prediction proved to be accurate.

Gwendolyn Brooks was born in Topeka, Kansas. She grew
up in Chicago, Illinois. Her parents didn't have much money.
Still, her home was a happy place.

Brooks' parents encouraged her to write. Her father sang
around the house. He recited poetry. Her mother made sure
Gwendolyn had paper and pencils. Later, as an adult, Brooks
wrote a poem called "Andre." In the poem, the boy dreamed he
could choose his parents. In the end, Andre "knew what
parents I would take . . . the ones I always had!"

3
6
15
24
36
45
52
62
71
81
88
97
107
117
129
139
148

As an adult, Brooks remembers what it's like to be a child. 160
For example, children love animals. Often, a child's pet seems 170
like a best friend. In a poem called "Vern," Brooks says, "A 182
pup's a good companion—if a pup you've got." 191

Children love nature. As a child, Gwendolyn liked to watch 201
the changing sky. As an adult, she describes the whiteness of 212
the snow. She notices the sounds, too. Her poem "Cynthia in 223
the Snow" begins, "It SUSHES." Did you ever see the word 234
sushes anywhere else? Probably not. Even so, it's just right for 245
the soft sounds you hear when snow is falling. 254

Children like to play. As a child, Brooks and her brother 265
Raymond played in the backyard. They made mud pies. They 275
played tag or hide-and-seek. Indoors, they played checkers or 284
dominoes. 285

Brooks still likes to play. Now she plays with words. She 296
says that the snow "laughs a lovely softness and whitely whirs 307
away." That's word play! 311

You can read Gwendolyn Brooks's poems in a book called 321
Bronzeville Boys and Girls. The poems tell about life in the 332
city. "Bronzeville" is like the Chicago neighborhood where 340
Brooks grew up. In the book, she wrote about children she 351
knew. Many of the poems are named for children—Mirthine, 361
Tawanda, Narcissa, Eppie, and Eldora. Even the names sound 370
like poetry! 372

Sequoya's New Alphabet

by Rob Howell

3

6

As a Cherokee child in Tennessee in the late 1700s, Sequoya was fascinated by what his people called the "talking leaves." They were referring to printed books that people read and the sheets of paper that people wrote messages on. The Cherokees at that time could not read or write.

The Job Begins

At an older age, Sequoya got the idea to create a special alphabet for his people. At first, he tried to give every word its own written symbol. But he soon realized there were just too many words to do that. So instead, he created a symbol for each sound in the Cherokee vocabulary.

Sequoya began working on his alphabet in 1809. It was a huge job that he finished 12 years later in 1821. In the end, he had created symbols for 86 different sounds. But would the Cherokee people accept this new kind of communication instead of speech?

17
27
38
48
56

59

71
84
95
107
113

124
138
148
156
159

Testing the Results

According to legend, Sequoya asked his daughter to model
how well his alphabet worked. A panel of Cherokee chiefs
privately told Sequoya what to write on paper. After Sequoya
wrote it, his daughter read it aloud easily. The chiefs were fully
convinced that the new alphabet was good.

Sequoya's alphabet was so simple that it could be learned in
just a few days. Those who learned it first were soon able to
teach it to others. Within just a few months, nearly all the
Cherokees in that region were able to read and write.

A Changed People

Sequoya's new alphabet allowed the Cherokees to record
information about their own nation. They were also able to use
the alphabet to publish books and newspapers in their own
language. Through his hard work, Sequoya helped his people
communicate with others.

Are You All Right?

by Patricia Walsh

4
7

I was a college student studying to be a computer engineer. 18
On January 17, 1994, I had just fallen asleep after studying late. 30
Suddenly, I was awakened by a California earthquake. 38

My house in Northridge trembled. My computer bounced on 47
the table. Cabinet doors swung open. They slammed shut and 57
swung open again. I rushed to the front door. I grabbed the 69
doorknob and was bumped back and forth against the door. I 80
pulled on the doorknob, but the shifting of the house jammed 91
the door. 93

A great tug and another roll of the floor made the door snap 106
open. Out in the street, bricks were flying as chimneys fell and 118
buildings collapsed. And then it was quiet. 125

I coughed as the dust in the air choked me. I stepped over 138
the rubble of fallen bricks and broken window glass. I picked 149
my way to the grocery store parking lot. The people in the 161
neighborhood always gathered in the lot whenever an 169
earthquake hit. It felt good to have other people nearby. 179

The dawn began to light the sky. I saw crumpled buildings 190
and a car crushed beneath a collapsed garage. I could see into 202
the house across the street. A bed, a table, and Japanese 213
posters on the wall were in plain sight. This was the home of 226
my elderly neighbor, Mrs. Kanamori. I panicked as I realized I 237
hadn't seen her in the parking lot. 244

"Where is Mrs. Kanamori?" I asked a neighbor. "Have you   254
seen her?" He shook his head no.   261

I walked up to her house. I stood in front of what had been   275
her front door. "Mrs. Kanamori," I called out. "Where are you?   286
Are you all right?" My only answer was another small tremor.   297

I called again. "Mrs. Kanamori, it's me Lily Ohira. Please   307
answer me." I resolved to find her.   314

"Here I am Lily," said a voice behind me. "I'm OK."   325

"I'm so glad to see you!" I said.   333

"I am worried about my daughter," said Mrs. Kanamori.   342

"Is she still in the house?" I asked.   350

"Oh no. She lives in Boston," said Mrs. Kanamori. "She will   361
see this on the news. She will be very concerned about me.   373
How will she know I'm OK? There is no long-distance phone   384
service."   385

"Oh, Mrs. Kanamori. I'm so sorry," I said. Mrs. Kanamori   395
began to cry softly.   399

Later that day, I returned home. Dishes were broken. The   409
furniture was overturned. I wondered if my computer   417
would work.   419

I turned it on. It hummed, and the monitor screen glowed a   431
welcome glow. I connected to the Internet. The Internet allows   441
computer users all over the world to talk to each other. An   453
aftershock shook the floor under my feet. "I hope my computer   464
doesn't disconnect," I said. My monitor flickered, but   472
everything stayed on.   475

Messages from all over the country flashed on my screen.   485
Long-distance phone calls could not get through to California,   495
but the Internet could. The Internet does not depend on long-   506
distance phone lines.   509

Many people wanted information about friends and   516
relatives. I wished I could help someone. I wish I knew how to   529
reach Mrs. Kanamori's daughter.   533

Then a message from Boston appeared on my computer   542
screen. "I can't reach my mother, Aiko Kanamori. She lives in   553
Northridge. Could someone find out of she is all right?"   563

"Here is someone I can help!" I thought. The message was   574
from Mrs. Kanamori's daughter.   578

I smiled as I tapped the keys on my keyboard. "I just spoke   591
with your mom. Her house is gone, but she is fine. She sends   604
her love to you."   608

Guide Dogs

by Susan Ring

Every day you see people leaving their houses, walking
down the street, running to catch the bus. Without thinking
about it much, people have always shopped at the store, jogged
in the park, and visited friends. But it is not as easy for blind
people to be mobile and do all those things. That's why they
need the help of guide dogs.

How do guide dogs know what to do? It takes a lot of
training and good communication between the owner and
the dog.

Guide Dog Puppies

Guide dogs are chosen when they are puppies, depending
on their size and how smart they are. These puppies are raised
in homes with people who take care of them until they are
about a year old. Like most dogs, they learn that there is no
wetting on the floor, no digging in the yard, and no nibbling
from dinner plates. They also learn the meaning of "yes," "no,"
"good dog," and "sit." In addition, these puppies go everywhere
with their family so they get used to many places. They get
used to loud sounds so they don't get scared if something drops
on the floor or if people are applauding at a play.

14
24
35
49
61
67
80
88
90
93
102
114
126
139
151
162
172
184
196
207

Training School

209

The dogs are trained to wear a harness so their owners can hold on to them. Blind people know when to cross a street by hearing the cars going by. Their dogs are trained to stop at each curb and to go across the street when they hear "forward." They learn not to move if it is not safe to do so. They learn to turn when told "right" or "left." And when they hear "hop-up," they walk faster or go up the curb.

221
234
247
258
274
285
293

After five or six months at school, the time comes for each dog and its new owner to meet.

305
312

A New Home

315

The blind person who will own a guide dog must also be trained for a few weeks on how to work with the dog. After that, the owner and guide dog begin a new life together.

327
340
351

Trust and good communication make this partnership work.

359

Can Windmills Talk?

by Allan Walldren

Do you know what a windmill is? Look at the picture
closely. It shows a windmill with its arms in four positions.
Most windmills have four arms. When the wind blows, it
turns those arms. This turns a big stone inside the mill. The
stone grinds grain. It turns the grain into flour. Farmers
bring their grain to the mill. The miller makes it into flour.
Then people bake bread with the flour. There are many
windmills like these in Holland.

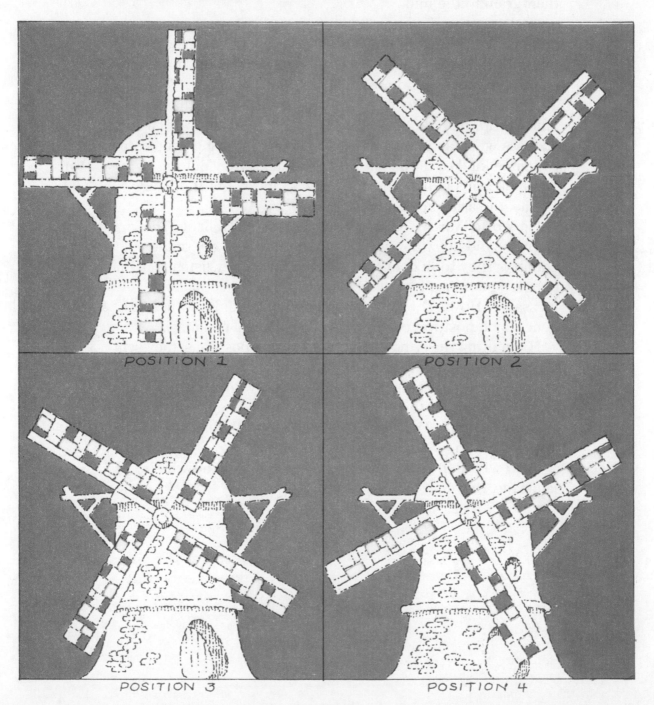

POSITION 1

POSITION 2

POSITION 3

POSITION 4

Do you think that windmills can talk? Well, they can. No, they don't speak words. Of course not. But they can talk with their arms. Here's how it works. 98 110 116

When the arms are not turning, the miller can leave them in any position. He can leave them in position 1. Or in position 2. Or in position 3. Or in position 4. Each position means something different. It's like hanging out a sign. It's a way of telling people about the mill. 128 141 152 164 169

Suppose the arms are in position 1. That shows that the mill is working. It has only stopped for a little while. Maybe the miller is having lunch. He'll be back soon. So farmers bring their grain to the mill. 181 193 204 209

But suppose the arms are in position 2. That shows that the mill is not working. It will be closed for a long time. Maybe the miller is ill. Maybe he has gone on a trip. Maybe the mill is broken. So farmers do not bring grain to that mill. 221 235 249 259

Perhaps you've seen a flag flying at half-mast. (That means halfway up the pole.) Flags are flown at half-mast to show sadness when an important person dies. In Holland people do the same kind of thing, but with windmills. They put the windmill arms in position 4 to show sadness. But for happy events, the arms are set in position 3. 269 280 290 301 312 320

In World War II, German soldiers invaded Holland. The Germans did not want any messages to be sent out of the country. They took over the radio stations. They listened in on people's phone calls. But the people of Holland still sent messages. How? They used their windmills. And they used a code. Each position of the arms had a special meaning. 329 341 352 362 372 382

By putting the windmill arms in certain positions, they sent messages to England. English pilots would fly over Holland. They would look at certain windmills. They knew the code. They could "read" the windmills' messages. They took the news back to England. The Germans didn't know about this code. They didn't know what was going on. 392 401 411 421 431 438

Can windmills talk? Indeed they can. If you know their language, they can tell you a lot. 448 455

The Beginning of Books

by Tara Lee

No one knows for sure when books first were produced.
Some historians believe that the earliest books may have been
written in Egypt around 4,700 years ago. The Egyptians wrote
on papyrus, a material from plants that grew along the Nile
River. The papyrus was pressed into a material to write on. It
was then rolled into long scrolls, which became the first books.
To read the scrolls, a person would unroll the scroll and roll it
onto another wooden dowel as they read. In fact, the word
paper comes from the Egyptian word *papyrus*.

Other Early Books

In Babylonia (now Iraq), people wrote by pressing marks
into small clay tablets. They used the tablets to record business
records, stories, and histories. Then they baked or dried the
clay to make it harder. About 3,000 years ago, the Chinese
made books by writing on long strips of wood or bamboo and
then tying them together. About 2,500 years ago, the ancient
Greeks used papyrus as their main writing material. They also
used wooden tablets covered with wax as notebooks.

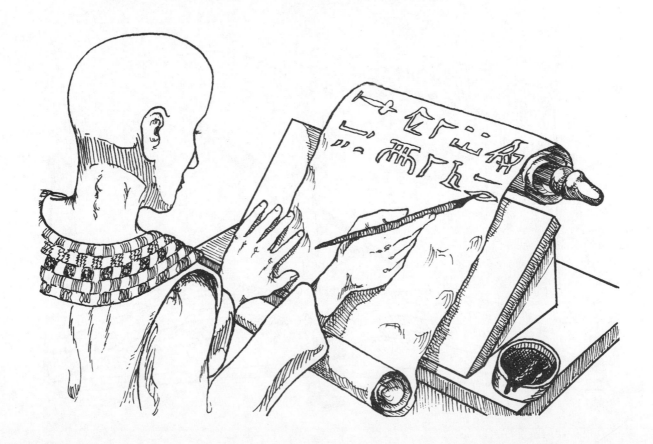

The Change to Parchment

In time, papyrus, clay, and wood were replaced with a newer writing material called parchment. Parchment was a special form of animal skin prepared for writing that was stronger and smoother than papyrus. It lasted longest of all the writing materials at that time. It also cost less than papyrus.

The First Bound Books

Around the year A.D. 300, the Romans invented a new type of book called the codex. Instead of using long parchment scrolls, they cut parchment into square, flat sheets. Next, they folded the sheets and sewed them along the edge. Then they would bind the pages with thin pieces of wood covered with leather.

A codex was easier to use than a scroll. A reader could open it to any page instead of winding and rewinding a scroll. A codex allowed more writing space because a person could write on both sides of the paper. Today, the codex is still the main form of books.

190
200
208
218
229
240
244
255
265
275
286
297
298
310
323
332
345
349

A Present for Nikko

by Judy Lloyd

When her father had promised a big surprise for her eleventh birthday, Nikko had never expected something like this! 18 26

"Nikko, I'd like you to meet Ardra," said her father. "Ardra is an android." 38 40

"Good morning, Nikko. I am very pleased to meet you." Ardra looked and sounded like a girl about Nikko's age. But her skin looked smooth and polished, almost like a pearl. Her green eyes seemed to reflect the light as she stared, unblinking, at Nikko. 51 63 74 85

"G-g-good morning," Nikko slowly stammered. 90

"As you can see," said Nikko's father, "Ardra speaks and understands English. But if you want her to do a task, you have to teach her. Happy birthday, sweetheart." 100 113 119

Nikko hugged her father and thanked him as he left for work. She was very excited. What fun it would be to teach her very own android. 130 143 146

Ardra waited quietly while Nikko thought about what she could have Ardra do. Perhaps she could get the android to help with her chores around the house. 155 167 173

"Come with me, please, Ardra," said Nikko, leading the way to her bedroom. 183 186

Nikko's poodle, Spike, sniffed curiously at Ardra, then trotted merrily behind her. 194 198

"First, I'll show you how to make the bed," announced Nikko. Ardra looked carefully around the bedroom, then became very still—staring straight ahead. Nikko knew that this was how an android "thought" about a command before acting. 208 216 226 236

Finally, Ardra spoke. "I cannot make a bed because I have   247
no wood. I also need nails and tools."   255

"No, I don't mean make a bed. I mean make *the* bed," said   268
Nikko patiently.   270

Ardra just stared at Nikko, unblinking. "That does not make   280
sense. They are the same."   285

Nikko decided to try something else. "I'll show you how to   296
clean up the room—is that OK?"   303

Ardra stared. "O—the fifteenth letter of the English   312
alphabet. K—the eleventh letter of the English alphabet."   321

"This isn't going to be as easy as I thought," muttered Nikko.   333
"Now watch, Ardra, and I'll show you exactly what to do."   344
Nikko picked up an armful of stuffed animals from the bed and   356
put them on a shelf. "Now you try it, Ardra."   366

The android looked around. Moving faster than Nikko   374
thought possible, Ardra scooped Spike into her arms. The dog   384
let out a startled yelp as Ardra dropped him onto the shelf next   397
to the stuffed animals.   401

"No, no!" cried Nikko, rescuing the whimpering poodle.   409

Ardra's green eyes never blinked. "I did exactly as you   419
showed me," she said calmly.   424

Nikko sighed. "Follow me to the kitchen, Ardra, and I'll   434
show you how to wash the dishes."   441

Ardra stared straight ahead. Nikko could almost hear her   450
circuits humming. "Wash—to clean, using water. I am not   460
programmed to wash dishes. My outer covering is not   469
waterproof. Water could rust my circuits."   475

Disgusted, Nikko said, "I suppose this means you'll be no   485
help at all with the chores. I thought that androids were   496
supposed to be smart."   500

Ardra's eyes seemed to twinkle and she blinked—just once.   510
"We are."   512

And for just a moment, Nikko was sure that she saw   523
Ardra smile.   525

Marcel Marceau

by James O'Neill

He's caught in a giant box and can't get out. He feels along   18
the sides and the top, but it's closed all the way around. Then   31
the box gets smaller and closes in on him more and more. There   44
isn't even a tiny hole for him to wriggle out of. Soon he must   58
stand with his arms flat against his sides. What happens now?   69

It's About Mime   72

What happens now is the lights come on, and the people   83
watching him cheer and clap their hands. But there isn't any   94
box. Instead, there's just a man named Marcel Marceau   103
pretending to be in a box. He is doing mime. Mime is a way of   118
telling a story without words. A mime tells everything by using   129
only his or her face and body. He uses hand movements, body   141
language, and different expressions on his face to tell a   151
complete story.   153

The Greatest Mime   156

Marcel Marceau is thought to be the greatest mime in the   167
world. Every little turn, every wrinkle in his face lets people   178
know his mood and his story. A mime can speak to anyone, no   191
matter where the person lives or what language the person   201
speaks.   202

Marcel Marceau was born in France. He wanted to be a   213
mime at a very young age and would imitate anything and   224
anyone he found interesting. He loved to watch silent movies   234
and the people who starred in them, like Charlie Chaplin. So he   246
decided to go to a special school and learn how to be a mime.   260

Bip Is Born   263

About 50 years ago, Marcel Marceau made up his most   273
famous character, a clown named Bip. Maybe you've seen   282
pictures of Bip in his striped shirt and tiny black hat. Bip can   295
make you believe anything just by the way he moves and looks.   307
And always, he is silent. He doesn't say anything.   316

You can watch him wrestle a lion, dance with a princess,   327
and jump onto a moving train. He'll pretend to climb steps that   339
don't end, and you'll think he's really climbing them. It's hard to   351
believe the only thing you're seeing is Marcel Marceau. He has   362
a wonderful imagination.   365

One Language   367

It's beyond words. It's beyond cities, towns, and countries.   376
A room filled with people who don't speak the same language   387
and who can't understand each other can watch Marcel   396
Marceau and know exactly what he's saying. And he does it all   408
in silence.   410

Nell's Big Day

by Bea Asasaki

The big day had come at last! Nell passed her swimming tests, and she had just turned twelve. That didn't seem like much, but it was. Nell's older sister, Ann, was a biologist with the Dolphin Research Center in Florida. Nell had watched Ann work with the dolphins many times. But Ann wouldn't let Nell go into the water with them until she was twelve. Today was the day!

"Which dolphins will I be swimming with, Ann?" Nell loved them all, but she had a couple of favorites.

Ann frowned, pretending to think about the choice. "Oh, I don't know. How about . . . Kikko and Max?"

"Yes!" cried Nell, punching the air with her fist. Nell helped Ann check the five pens. The dolphins really lived in the ocean, but were separated from the open sea by low wire fences.

"I can't believe that they don't jump the fences and swim   156
away," said Nell.   159

"Oh, they take off from time to time," explained Ann, "but   170
they always come back." She picked up a bucket of fish and   182
walked toward the farthest pen.   187

Nell laughed. "They probably stick around for the free fish."   197

Nell yelled a good morning greeting to Kikko and Max. They   208
responded with a lively chorus of clicks and whistles.   217

"Looks like they're ready to play," said Ann, as the two   228
dolphins leaped high out of the water. "Do you remember the   239
signals, Nell?"   241

"Hah," said Nell, slipping quickly out of her sandals. "I've   251
been doing them in my sleep!"   257

Nell jumped into the water and swam a few strokes away   268
from the dock. Then, as she'd seen Ann do many times, she   280
slapped the surface a few times. Max's sleek, gray dorsal fin   291
surfaced just behind her. Nell cupped her hand around the front   302
of the fin. She whooped in delight as the dolphin towed her   314
quickly through the water.   318

"Wow!" she cried, letting go as Max dove beneath the   328
surface. "He's fast!"   331

Ann laughed, watching as Max surfaced for his fishy   340
reward. He seemed very proud of himself, bobbing his head   350
and chattering his own praises.   355

Nell rolled onto her back in the center of the pen, floating   367
quietly. In the next instant, Kikko's huge form leaped in a   378
graceful arc over Nell's body.   383

Nell played with her friends for a while longer. Then,   393
holding onto the dock with one hand, she tapped her cheek   404
with her finger. Kikko rose from the water and touched her   415
nose gently to Nell's cheek—a kiss good-bye.   423

When Nell climbed from the water, Kikko and Max whistled   433
and chirped, as if they didn't want her to leave. She threw them   446
each another fish and promised to return.   453

"They're so smart," she told Ann. "It's as if they really   464
understand what I say."   468

"They know at least thirty words of English, Nell. And we   479
don't understand a single word of dolphin. Maybe dolphins are   489
smarter than people!"   492

They both laughed, but Nell couldn't help but wonder.   501

Spreading the News

by Daniel Washington

3
6

Scooter was very excited when he awoke Saturday morning. He was planning to produce a one-man circus in his yard for his friends the next afternoon.

At breakfast, Scooter ate with Aunt Arlene, who was visiting.

"Will there be a large group of children at your circus?" she asked, helping herself to some potatoes.

"I'm not sure," Scooter said. "I have to invite everyone today." He took two spoonfuls of eggs.

"Today?" Aunt Arlene cried. "Isn't that a little late for a show that's tomorrow? I think you should have spread the news earlier."

"But I've been too busy practicing," Scooter said. "You should see my juggling act! Plus I taught my pet poodle to jump through hoops! This afternoon I'll phone everyone and ask them to come."

"But haven't you heard?" Aunt Arlene said. "The phone lines are down today due to a cable problem. So you can't call your friends."

15
28
32
41
42
54
60
70
77
89
99
100
109
122
131
134
144
157
158

"Then I know!" Scooter cried. "I'll go to Dad's office and use his fax machine." 170 173

"That won't work," Aunt Arlene explained. "First, his office is closed today. Second, if the phone lines aren't working, the fax machine won't work, either. And besides, I doubt that all your friends have fax machines of their own to get your message." 182 193 204 215 216

"That's true," Scooter sighed. "So what should I do?" 225

"Well," Aunt Arlene smiled, "before telephones and fax machines, there was pony express. Mail was delivered by their riders." 233 243 244

"We don't have ponies!" Scooter laughed. 250

"True," his aunt said, "but we do have our bicycles. Let's bike around town and deliver your circus invitations in person! It beats using your feet." 261 271 276

That afternoon, the two rode on their bicycles, spreading the news. 285 287

"Sometimes," Aunt Arlene laughed, "the old-fashioned ways are still the best!" 294 298

The Missing Maps

by Gary Drury

Mai opened one eye. Tetra's two suns shone through the bedroom window of the space station. She could hear her family stirring. It was time to get up. Then she heard a loud cry. 16 26 40

Mai jumped out of bed. She ran to the meeting room in the middle of the station. Her parents and other families were there. Grace, the station's clerk, came out of the vault. 53 63 73

"The safe is open, and the maps are missing!" she cried. 84

"The maps to the new mines?" Mai's father asked. "The entire colony needs those maps!" 94 99

It was true. Mai's father, Captain Tanaka, had led the search for new sources of food. When the space station workers had discovered the mines, the entire colony was excited. The mines held large amounts of Agra, a substance that could be transformed into food. Now the colony had enough food for hundreds of years. 110 121 131 141 151 154

"Why would anyone take the maps?" Mai asked. 162

"The Agra would make a person very rich," her father answered. "Whoever took those maps isn't thinking about the colony." Captain Tanaka looked around the room. "This is a closed station, so whoever opened that safe is with us now." 172 181 191 202

The families looked at one another. No one could believe that one of their own would be that selfish. 212 221

"Will someone make that Cyborg be quiet?" Grace asked. 230

"That's right," Mai thought. "Where was the Cyborg during the night?" 239 241

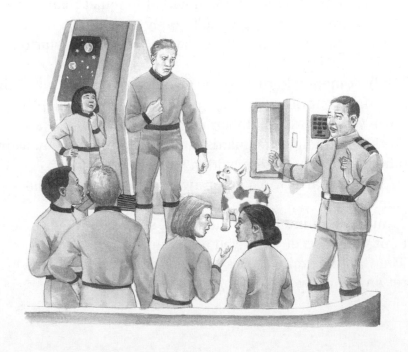

The Cyborg was a doglike creature. Its job was to guard the   253
vault. If anyone came near the room, it began to whine loudly.   265
The creature had been crying since Grace first screamed.   274

"I'll settle it down." Tabor, the Cyborg's trainer, stepped   283
forward. He walked into the room that held the safe. "Easy,   294
now." Tabor patted the creature's head, and it quieted down   304
right away.   306

Captain Tanaka said, "Everyone! Think about where you   314
were last night. Write the name of anyone who saw you on a   327
piece of paper, and give the paper to me."   336

Grace looked at Captain Tanaka. "Are you going to explain   346
what you were doing? I'm sure everyone will want to know."   357

Grace knew that much of Captain Tanaka's job was secret.   367
No one was sure what he did. Captain Tanaka said nothing. He   379
just smiled at Grace. "Let's get started, shall we?" he said.   390

Mai knew the others were thinking about her father. Could   400
he have taken the maps? Or what about Grace? She had found   412
the safe open.   415

"I'd better think about where I was," Mai said.   424

Mai had retired after reading some reports. She had seen no   435
one. She fell deeply asleep. Nothing had awakened her. Mai   445
thought and thought about that night. Then she had an idea.   456
She found her father and told him.   463

One hour later, Captain Tanaka assembled the families   471
together.   472

"We have news," he began. "At this moment, Tabor's room is   483
being searched."   485

"What?" said Tabor. "Why?"   489

"My daughter pointed out one interesting fact about last   498
night," the captain said. "It was quiet. More quiet than usual.   509
Why? Because the Cyborg wasn't crying or whining. If anyone   519
had tried to open the safe, the creature would have started   530
crying."   531

"Only someone known to the Cyborg could have taken the   541
maps," Mai went on. "The only person who could quiet the   552
creature was its trainer, Tabor."   557

At that moment, two guards entered the room. They were   567
holding maps. "They were hidden in the floor, Captain."   576

After the guards took Tabor away, Grace spoke to the   586
captain.   587

"You have an intelligent daughter," she said. "Maybe she can   597
find out what secret work you are doing."   605

The Captain smiled. "But, Grace, then it wouldn't be a   615
secret anymore, would it?"   619

The First American Settlers

by Maria Diaz

4

7

Long before any Europeans arrived in North America, people were living there. Scientists believe these people came from Asia thousands of years ago. At the time, much of the earth that is now under water was dry land. So people may have walked across land that once joined Asia and North America. Today water covers that land.

Many Peoples, Many Ways

The first Americans were not one group of people. They were many different groups. They spoke their own languages and led their own ways of life. Some lived in cities, and some lived in villages. Others kept moving all year, hunting animals and picking wild plants. The Aztec and Maya of Central America lived in large cities with as many as 100,000 people.

In eastern North America, Native Americans lived in small villages and farmed. They grew corn, beans, and squash. In South America, the Native Americans lived in small groups and ate mainly fish and berries.

15
24
36
48
58
64
68
78
87
100
110
120
131
140
150
160
165

The Spanish Arrive 168

Around 1500, the Spanish started arriving in North America. 177
At first, the Native Americans and the Spanish helped one 187
another. The Native Americans taught the Spanish how to 196
survive. They showed them how to travel by canoe and offered 207
them new foods, like peanuts, potatoes, corn, and tomatoes. In 217
return, the Spanish gave the Native Americans metal tools, 226
cattle, and horses. 229

Then things began to change. The Spanish and the Native 239
Americans had very different ways of life. They didn't 248
understand each other's ways of doing things. The Spanish also 258
wanted the new lands and riches for themselves. Soon they 268
were fighting each other. 272

The battling continued as the English, the Dutch, and other 282
Europeans came to North America. By the time it all ended, 293
millions of Native Americans had died from disease and war. 303
Others had lost all their lands. 309

Language, Culture, and Tradition 313

We have much to thank the first Americans for. More than 324
half the states have Native American names. Hundreds of 333
mountains, rivers, and cities do, too. Many words we use are 344
Native American, like canoe, toboggan, and skunk. We eat 353
tomatoes, peanuts, beans, squash, and corn. Native Americans 361
first grew these foods. Most importantly, we are learning to 371
respect and protect nature as they did. 378

Today, we all join Native Americans in celebrating their 387
traditions and beliefs. By doing so, we honor and remember the 398
first Americans. 400

Phillis Wheatley: The Slave Poet

5

Should you wonder why I love freedom so— 13
I, young in life, was snatched from my African home. 23
I pray others never feel the sorrow and misery I have known. 35

These lines are from a poem by Phillis Wheatley. She wrote 46
them more than two hundred years ago. 53

Phillis was born in 1753 in Senegal, West Africa. When she 64
was eight, she was brought to Boston on a slave ship. Small, 76
sick, and scared, she was sold at a public auction. A man 88
named John Wheatley bought her. He wanted a female slave to 99
help his wife and their daughter, Mary. He gave Phillis their 110
family name. People who bought slaves often did this. 119

Phillis was to be a house slave. She was taught the 130
household chores. But the Wheatleys were kind to Phillis. They 140
treated her like part of the family. Young Mary helped her learn 152
English. Phillis learned quickly. Soon she could read the Bible. 162
She also read myths, poems, and any classics she found in the 174
house. Some people would not believe that a black slave girl 185
could read. Many slave owners felt slaves should not even be 196
allowed to read. 199

Once she could read, Phillis was eager to learn how to   210
write. John Wheatley said, "As to her writing, her own curiosity   221
led her to it. And she learned in so short a time!" Phillis wrote   235
her first story when she was twelve. Here is part of it: 247

Today I saw the morning glories wake. Of all the flowers   258
in the garden, they are my dearest. They are the children of   270
the sun. When the sun sets, they bow their heads and go to   283
sleep. What else can they do when the sun is gone? The world   296
is dark. They cannot see. But when the sun comes up again   308
they lift their heads and smile. Their faces are glad.   318

Phillis learned the Latin language. She translated Latin   326
poems into English. When she was thirteen, she had a new   337
idea. She would write poems of her own.   345
In those days, writers often read their works in public.   355
People would gather at the church to hear Phillis read her   366
poems. She became known around Boston. People invited her   375
to their homes to read her latest work.   383
In October 1775, Phillis wrote a poem about George   392
Washington. It praised his courage and strength. She sent the   402
poem to him. Four months passed. At last, Washington   411
answered Phillis. He apologized that it had taken so long to   422
write back. He said that he liked her poem very much. He   434
thought she had talent. He even invited her to visit him.   445
Phillis was thrilled to get Washington's letter. But she felt   455
even more proud that April. *The Pennsylvania Magazine*   463
printed her George Washington poem along with the letter   472
Washington had written to her. Now, people beyond Boston   481
learned of the slave poet.   486
Soon after, Phillis became ill. A doctor thought that she   496
should get away from the city. He said an ocean voyage might   508
help her regain her health. So Phillis traveled to England.   518
People welcomed her there. They asked her to read her poems   529
at small parties held especially for her.   536
Phillis returned to Boston. She was no longer a slave. She   547
married and had three children. But she was very poor for the   559
rest of her life. She died at the young age of thirty-one.   571
Phillis Wheatley had many hard times. But she   579
accomplished a great deal in her short life. She would be proud   591
to know that she is still remembered today.   599

A Child's Life in Colonial Days

by Susan Shafer

What was it like to be a boy or girl during the Colonial period of this country? That was the time from about 1600 to 1776. Then, America was made up of different territories. It was even before the colonies had become the 13 original states of the United States.

Life during Colonial times was not easy. There were always chores to be done, like milking cows or planting seeds. Often the work was difficult and boring. But children back then did two things that children do today. They went to school and worked hard, but they also played games.

School Days

In school, boys and girls learned some of the same things children learn today—reading, writing, and arithmetic. Some of the boys might later study to become doctors or lawyers. But girls were expected to be homemakers.

For boys, and girls too, teachers were strict. Students who did not pay attention were sent to sit in the corner of the room. Children who could not keep quiet were given a stick, called a whispering stick, to hold between their teeth. A child couldn't talk without dropping the stick from his or her mouth.

22
34
45
56
59
69
80
91
102
109
111
122
131
142
148
158
172
184
194
204

Fun and Games

Back in Colonial days, children played many of the same games children play today: hide-and-seek, tag, hopscotch, and leapfrog. These games not only were fun, but also they made children fit. They taught skills such as how to aim, how to problem solve, and how to follow rules. By playing games, children also learned to be courteous and to get along with their friends, brothers, and sisters. Since families in Colonial times often had six, seven, or eight children, that was important.

There weren't any toy stores back in the Colonial period, so children learned to make their own toys. Using cotton, rags, and corn husks, they made toy dolls or animals. Also, children used string, bits of cloth, and pieces of wood to make kites.

On cold winter nights, Colonial families would sit around the fireplace to stay warm. They would try saying tongue twisters fast. One was, "She sheared six shabby sick sheep." Children also asked each other clever riddles, such as "What kind of room is not in a house?" (a mushroom)

Life for Colonial children was hard. But there was always time for learning and for fun.

207
217
225
236
248
258
269
278
288
289
300
310
321
333
342
352
362
372
382
392
398

The Clever Whitewasher

3

adapted from *The Adventures of Tom Sawyer* by Samuel Clemens

13

Samuel Clemens, who wrote under the name "Mark Twain," created one of the first realistic books for and about children. It is The Adventures of Tom Sawyer, *published in 1876. It describes life in a small American town more than a century ago. This story comes from one of its best-known chapters.*

21
32
42
53
65
66

It was a bright, fresh Saturday in summer. But Tom Sawyer could take no pleasure in it, for he had to whitewash his Aunt Polly's board fence. He stood on the sidewalk with a bucket of whitewash and a long-handled brush. As he examined the huge length of fence, his heart sank.

77
90
102
113
119

He dipped his brush and passed it along the highest plank. Comparing this small whitewashed area with the vast continent of fence that remained, he sat down, feeling hopeless.

130
139
148

Jim came by, on his way to get water.

157

"Say, Jim, I'll get your water if you'll whitewash some."

167

"Can't," said Jim. "Your Aunt Polly told me you'd ask, but she said I mustn't."

178
182

"I'll give you a white marble," Tom said. The offer was attractive, but Jim resisted.

193
197

"I'll show you my sore toe besides," Tom added.

206

Jim was won over. But just then Aunt Polly appeared and sent Jim about his business.

217
222

Tom thought of all the things he'd rather be doing and began to search his pockets for toys, marbles, and other things he might use to pay other boys to do his work. But there wasn't nearly enough.

234
245
258
260

Then inspiration struck! 263

Tom took up his brush and went back to work. Soon Ben 275
Rogers came into view, eating an apple. Tom paid no attention. 286
He just kept painting, with a satisfied look. 294

"Got to work, huh?" 298

"Ben!" exclaimed Tom, acting surprised. "I didn't notice you." 307

"I'm going swimming," said Ben. "Don't you wish *you* could? 317
Too bad you've got to work!" Ben teased. 325

"What do you call work?" 330

"Isn't *that* work?" said Ben. 335

"Well, maybe it's work and maybe not," said Tom. "All I 346
know is, it suits me fine!" 352

"Come on," said Ben. "You don't mean you *like* it?" 362

"Like it? Why shouldn't I? Does a boy get a chance to 374
whitewash a fence every day?" 379

Well, Ben hadn't thought of it that way. 387

Tom swept his brush back and forth. Now and then he'd 398
step back and admire his work. Then he'd add a little touch and 411
study the result. 414

Ben watched every move. 418

"Say, Tom, let *me* whitewash a little." 425

Tom thought for a moment. "No, no, it wouldn't do. Aunt 436
Polly's very particular about this fence. It's got to be done just 448
so. There's very few boys can do it right." 457

"I'll bet *I* can. Just let me *try*. I'll be careful." 468

"Well . . . No, Ben, I'd like to—I really would—but what if 480
something bad happened?" 483

"I'll give you my apple," Ben said. 490

With an unwilling face but a cheerful heart, Tom gave up the 502
brush, and Ben began to whitewash. 508

Tom sat in the shade, munching Ben's apple and plotting 518
how to trap other boys. When Ben was worn out, there was no 531
lack of others to take his place. Each one would begin by 543
jeering, but soon Tom had him begging for a chance to 554
whitewash. And Tom soon had a growing pile of treasures, too. 565
Boys traded all kinds of things for the privilege of 575
whitewashing—chalk, a kite, a dog collar 582

While Tom sat idle, the fence got three coats of whitewash. 593

Aunt Polly was amazed at the finished job. 601

And Tom? He had discovered a great fact of human nature: 612
To make a person really want something, you need only make it 624
hard to get. And something else: Work is anything you *have* to 636
do; play is anything you *don't have* to do. 645

A Visit to Williamsburg

by Susan Ring

4

7

I just got back from the best trip I have ever taken. My family and I visited Williamsburg, Virginia. In Williamsburg, I felt as if I had gone back in time. The whole town is set up the way it was during the 1700s, when it was the capital of the Virginia colony. Many of the old buildings were saved, and they still look like they did back then. Even the people working there dress the way people did in the 1700s. They also go about life as if they were living in the 1700s.

A Look at Colonial Life

First, we watched a woman spin wool from sheep that were outside in the field. Someone told me that kind of sheep is very rare now, but they were plentiful in Colonial America. The woman sat at an old spinning wheel. There was a big basket of wool next to her on the floor. She wrapped the wool around the wheel and then made it move by pressing her foot up and down on a pedal. She couldn't plug it in because back then there wasn't any electricity. The woman told me that she was making a blanket to use during the winter. It must have been very cold during the winter in the 1700s. The only source of heat the Colonists had in their houses came from the fireplace.

20
29
45
58
69
80
93
102
107
118
131
141
154
167
180
192
203
216
228
237

Colonial Children   239

    Even back then, children played with many different types   248
of toys. They had dolls and drums and wooden animals. In   259
Williamsburg, we saw children playing marbles and hopscotch.   267
Also, there was a boy walking on stilts, two wooden poles that   279
he wore on his feet to make himself taller. In the schoolhouse, I   292
saw an old sign in the classroom that showed the alphabet. Did   304
you know that they didn't use the letters *j* and *u*?   315

Making Things   317

    The Colonial Americans had to make just about everything   326
because there weren't any stores where they could buy what   336
they needed. We saw some people making nice candles. They   346
dipped string into hot wax to make the candles.   355

    Another man was making cups out of silver. He was the   366
silversmith, and he also made other utensils, like spoons, forks,   376
and plates. In another building, we saw a woman and her six   388
children making wreaths for the holidays. Then we saw someone   398
making wigs for men, like the one George Washington wore.   408

Going Home   410

    I found out that all of these people don't really live in   422
Williamsburg. They just work there. At the end of the day, they   434
change their clothes and go home. It seems really fun. I'd like   446
to work in Williamsburg someday, too.   452

She Was First

by Carol A. Josel

Annie Smith Peck was fifty-eight years old that September 2, 1909. It was a Wednesday. The time was three-thirty in the afternoon, to be exact. There she stood. She felt as if she were standing on the top of the world. She and her two guides, Rudolph Tangwalder and Gabriel Zumtaugwald, had made it. They stood on the pointed tip of Mount Huascarán (Hwah scah RAHN) in Peru. It is one of the highest mountains in the world. No one had ever stood there before. Peck finally had done it!

For the first time in her life Peck felt afraid. She had reached the top. But would she live to tell anyone of her adventure? It did not seem likely. The wild wind made the cold seem even stronger. The blowing snow was blinding. Quickly Peck took pictures in each of the four directions. The storm was growing worse. Soon it would be dark. The wind and thin air made speaking impossible. So they started back down.

Their small camp was about 2000 feet below. The cold was already a problem. Peck had lost one of her gloves on the way up. The storm kept getting worse. Would they make it? Foot by foot, they climbed down the mountain. Many times they slipped and slid. Finally they reached the tents.

Who was this woman who climbed mountains, wrote books, taught school, and gave talks?

Annie Smith Peck was born in Rhode Island on October 19, 1850. Her parents raised her to be a lady. In those times, ladies and gentlemen were taught different things. Like all the girls she knew, she learned to sew and play the piano. But she wanted more. She loved sports. She made her brothers teach her games. She believed she could do anything boys could do. She was right. Her parents never stood in her way. But it was often hard for them to understand her.

At twenty-two, Peck finished school. She then became a teacher. But that was not enough. Soon she learned that the University of Michigan was now open to women. So she went there. She wanted an education just like her brothers'. At Michigan she earned it. She then went on to teach Latin at Purdue University.

16
28
41
53
61
72
85
97
109
121
133
142
153
165
174
185
198
210
220
227
236
241
251
264
274
287
297
308
321
328
337
348
359
369
381
383

Then Peck took a year off. She visited Europe. She saw the 395
Matterhorn for the first time. The mountain seemed to call to 406
her. Now she had something new to try for. To climb, though, 418
she needed money. 421

So Annie Smith Peck wrote speeches and spoke to large 431
crowds of people who paid money to hear her ideas. She spoke 443
about the rights of women to make history just as men do. As 456
she said, everyone needs important work to do. Climbing 465
mountains that have never been climbed was going to be her 476
important work. Soon Peck had raised enough money to stop 486
teaching school. She could start climbing. 492

Peck was not the first woman to climb the Matterhorn. But 503
how she did it made a difference from those other women 514
climbers. They had worn long skirts. Peck put on loose-fitting 524
trousers and a long shirt. She had heavy boots and a hat. In that 538
costume she climbed mountain after mountain. Each one was 547
higher than the last. By 1900, she had climbed twenty of them. 559
But even this was not enough. 565

Peck wanted to climb a mountain no one—man or woman— 576
had ever climbed. In the end she picked Huascarán, a great 587
mountain in Peru. Five times she tried. Five times she failed. 598
Either frightened guides or bad weather drove her back. Most 608
people would have given up, but not Peck. In 1909, she and two 621
guides climbed into history. 625

History would have remembered Peck even if she had not 635
climbed mountains. Her work for women's rights helped many 644
people see that everyone must be treated fairly. One of the 655
happiest days in her life was when she was sixty-seven years 666
old. That day she voted for the first time. 675

But Peck kept climbing mountains long after that. At the 685
age of eighty-two she climbed Mount Madison in New 694
Hampshire. And it is for mountain climbing that Annie Smith 704
Peck is best remembered. After all, she was, and still is, the 716
only woman in history to have been the first to reach the top of 730
one of the world's highest mountains. 736

Lewis and Clark

by Katharine Stevens

New Expedition

In 1803, Congress approved President Thomas Jefferson's plan for exploring the Missouri and Columbia Rivers. Jefferson wanted to know if Americans could travel west to the Pacific Ocean following these rivers. He needed a brave and strong man to lead the trip. Jefferson asked his secretary-aide and former Army captain, Meriwether Lewis, if he would lead the expedition. Lewis was happy to go but felt that this would be a very challenging job, and he would need help. He knew that the right person to help him was his old friend and former commanding officer, William Clark.

Who Were Lewis and Clark?

Lewis and Clark were both intelligent, adventurous, and courageous and shared a deep respect for each other. Lewis was born in Virginia in 1774 and grew up as a neighbor of Thomas Jefferson. As a boy, Lewis spent many hours exploring the woods and gaining knowledge of plants and animals. In 1801, Lewis was an Army captain when he received a letter from Thomas Jefferson offering him a position as his secretary-aide.

Clark was also born in Virginia, in 1770, and was one of ten children. His family later moved to Kentucky where they were one of the earliest settlers. Clark was a lieutenant when Lewis joined the army in 1794.

8
15
24
35
45
55
65
77
89
101
105
110
118
128
140
150
159
170
181
182
195
205
216
221

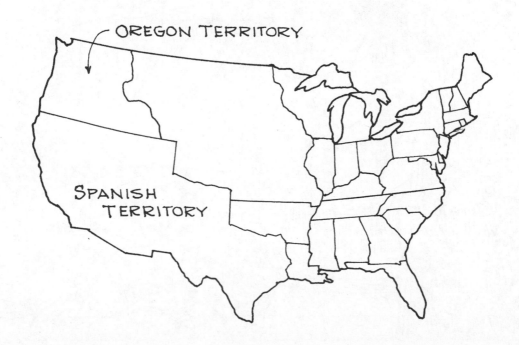

The Long Journey 224

Their trip began with a few boats and about 45 men, sailing 236
on the Missouri River and heading for the Pacific Ocean. No 247
one knew if they would make it back home alive. They also saw 260
wildlife that was new to them, such as coyotes and prairie 271
dogs. Lewis took many notes about the plants and animals they 282
saw. Clark knew the land and drew maps of where they went. 294

During their journey, there were many hard times, too. The 304
men hunted and fished but couldn't always find food. Some 314
Native Americans along the way were friendly, but others were 324
not so friendly. Lewis and Clark and their men spent the winter 336
with a group of Native Americans and became friends with a 347
woman named Sacagawea (ˌsa-kə-jə-ˈwē-ə). When spring came, 353
Sacagawea went with them and helped them find their way, 363
speak to Native Americans, and learn which wild roots and 373
fruits could be eaten. 377

After about a year, Lewis and Clark finally got to the Pacific 389
Ocean. Then they had to turn around and go all the way back to 403
the East again. 406

Welcome Home 408

Lewis and Clark came home safely more than two years 418
after they had begun their journey. Even today we think of 429
them as heroes. It was their long and brave trip that opened up 442
the American West for all of us. 449

Sitting Bull: Great Sioux Chief

by LaVere Anderson

2

5

8

The Sioux boy lay asleep under a cottonwood tree on the bank of the Grand River. He was alone and far from his village. All morning he had hunted with a bow and arrow through the summer woods, but he had not seen one rabbit or squirrel. At last, hot and tired, he had lain down to rest. His eyes grew heavy. He fell asleep. 19 32 44 56 69 73

The boy's name was Slow. Someday, when he was older and had done brave deeds, his father would give him another name. Now he was twelve, and he was called Slow because he took time to think before he acted. A boy needed to think carefully and be on his guard in the Dakota country in 1843. In such a wild land, there were many dangers. 84 95 107 119 133 139

Slow awoke with a start. Overhead, he heard a tapping. 149

He looked up and saw a yellow bird sitting on the branch of the cottonwood tree. It was a little yellowhammer, and it tapped the branch sharply with its beak. Tap—tap! Tap—tap! 162 172 183

"Your noise awoke me," Slow scolded the bird. 191

While he lay there, he heard another noise. Something was crashing through the woods. Suddenly, from out of the trees came a great brown grizzly bear. 201 211 217

Slow knew it was no use to fight. His small arrows were not made to go through a grizzly's thick fur and tough layers of fat. It was no use to run. A grizzly could run faster than a grown man. It was no use to jump into the river. A grizzly could swim. It was no use to climb the cottonwood. A grizzly could climb any tree that would hold its weight. 230 243 257 271 283 290

No, Slow thought, it was no use to do anything except lie still. Sometimes, a grizzly would not attack one who played dead. Slow shut his eyes and played dead. 302 312 320

On came the bear, right up to the boy, who hardly dared breathe. The bear nosed Slow's moccasins. It sniffed his bare legs. 332 341 343

Although he could not see the bear, Slow knew how   353
fearsome it looked. Its huge paws were strong enough to crush   364
a horse's skull with one blow.   370

Slow felt the grizzly's hot breath on his face. Then noisily as 382
it had come, the bear left. Slow opened one eye a little and   395
watched it go, swinging its head from side to side as it tried to 409
catch a scent on the air. He lay still until he could no longer 423
hear it crashing through the dark woods.   430

At last he sat up. The yellow bird looked down from its   442
branch, and Slow looked back. He knew that the bird had saved   454
his life by waking him with its tapping. Suddenly he felt a great 467
love for the tiny creature.   472

"Pretty yellow bird, I will never forget you," he said softly.   483
"All my life I will be a friend to all Bird People because of you." 498

Then the boy picked up his bow and arrows and started for   510
the circle of tepees that made up his village. He would have   522
exciting news to tell about the grizzly and about his new   533
friends the Bird People.   537

Slow found his father sitting with other men planning a   547
buffalo hunt. Like all Plains Indians, the Sioux depended on the 558
buffalo for food and other needs.   564

When the men had finished talking, Slow told Jumping Bull   574
about the grizzly.   577

"You acted wisely, my son," his father said. All the men   588
nodded. "Slow thinks before he acts," they agreed.   596

That night Slow sat with the other children at the evening   607
campfire. They listened to their elders tell hero tales of Sioux 618
history—tales of great deeds that the nation had done in the   630
past. The council fire was like a schoolroom for the children.   641
There they learned how to grow up to be good Sioux.   652

Overhead, a round yellow moon shone down on the Sioux   662
village. It lighted the smiling face of the boy who did not know he 676
would grow up to be the wisest man of all his people.   688

The Town Crier

by Debra Lowery

Rebecca carefully observed as Ben Franklin started up his printing press. He cranked the machine's large handle, and the daily newspaper began appearing, one sheet at a time.

"I love this printing press," Franklin remarked. "It's so much easier than employing a town crier."

Rebecca had a puzzled look on her face. "What's a town crier?" she asked.

Franklin chuckled. "That was before your time, Rebecca, and actually, before my time, too. You see, before 1704, there weren't any regular newspapers in the colonies. Imagine, no newspapers until 26 years ago!"

"How did people get their news before that?" Rebecca asked.

"That was the town crier's job," Franklin explained. "He marched from street corner to street corner, shouting out the day's important official messages. It was a hard job that required lots of time and energy."

15
25
34
44
50
61
64
72
83
92
97
106
107
116
126
136
142

"It sounds like fun to me!" Rebecca cried. "Everyone would   152
be listening to my every word."   158

Both Rebecca and Franklin began laughing. Just then they   167
heard a sharp, harsh noise from the printing press. The   177
machine suddenly came to a grinding halt.   184

"Oh, no!" Franklin sighed. "The press has stopped working   193
again, today of all days, when I need to publicize news of an   206
embargo against England. The embargo forbids all English   214
ships from entering the harbor. But no one will know about it   226
until tomorrow because it will take the remainder of the day to   238
fix the machine."   241

"I know what we can do!" Rebecca shouted. "Let me be the   253
town crier. Tell me exactly what to say, and I'll shout out   265
the news."   267

Franklin scribbled the message on paper. Rebecca departed   275
the shop and soon was standing on a major street corner   286
in town.   288

"Embargo against England!" she shouted proudly. "Come   295
and hear the latest news!"   300

A Festival of Crows

by Anne Kemmerle

People everywhere love to celebrate. Across the world 15
every year, thousands of celebrations occur in festivals or fairs. 25
In North America alone, there are music festivals, art festivals, 35
riverboat festivals, sweet-corn festivals, and pumpkin festivals. 43
One of the largest, best-known festivals is the Crow Indian Fair 55
and Rodeo in southern Montana. 60

Late in August every year, the Crow Indians gather in the 71
valley of the Little Big Horn River. They come from all over 83
their Montana reservation. About a mile from the site where the 94
Battle of Little Big Horn took place, the Crow put up their 106
tepees. Joining the Crow are many Blackfoot, Blood, Cree, and 116
Shoshone Indians. Other Native Americans join them, too. 124
Some travel from as far south as Mexico. They all come 135
together for a week of dancing, parades, and rodeos. 144

The Crow work hard getting ready for their big fair. In fact, 156
as soon as each year's fair ends, they start planning for the next 169
year's fair. 171

The Crow women begin by making native costumes. They 180
make shirts, dresses, and moccasins. Pieces of buckskin 188
become hair ties, belts, and purses. Later the women add 198
colored beads to the costumes. A few women know how to 209
make shapes with the beads. Carefully taking just one bead at a 221
time, they tie the beads to the buckskin. 229

In July, Crow families go to the mountains to cut lodgepole 240
pine trees. These pines have soft, light wood. Before the 250
trees dry out, the Crow strip the branches. Then they peel off 262
the bark. The wood is then used to make tall, straight poles 274
for tepees. 276

Many of the lodgepoles are used to set up the Crow's camp. 288
First they build a long open-air arbor. Straight posts going up 299
and down make the sides. Poles that cross each other make a 311
flat roof. Leafy branches piled on top finish the arbor. Inside, 322
each family finds a spot for its tables, tubs, and beds. 333

Along the outside of the arbor, the Crow put up their tepees. 345
For each tepee, four of the biggest poles are stood on their 357
ends, a few feet apart. Then the tops of these poles are tied 370
together. Finally the Crow put heavy cloth over the poles. They 381
fix the top so it will open or close. What a sight all these tepees 396
make! In fact, because so many Native Americans camp there 406
each year, the Crow Indian Fair is called the "Tepee Capital of 418
the World." 420

Most mornings at the fair begin with the Parade Dance. 430
Everyone dresses in native costume. The long parade through 439
the camp is a special kind of ceremony. The colors and shapes 451
show the Crows strong ties to the animal world. 460

Every afternoon brings the all-Indian rodeo. People from 468
almost every tribe in the U.S. and Canada compete in the 479
contests. There is horse racing, too, which has long been a 490
favorite sport of the Crow. 495

At dark, drums and songs call everyone to the dance arbor. 506
The Crow might begin the dance with the Men's and Women's 517
Traditional Dance. Soon members of other tribes are called to 527
join in. Through their costumes and their motion, the dancers 537
show the different ways of their tribes. They dance about ten 548
songs in a row, each song faster than the one before. 559

On the last night of the fair, the dancers, drummers, and 570
singers perform all night long. They finish with the Dance 580
Around the Camps. Only the Crow Indians take part in this 591
special dance. It shows the flight of the eagle, a bird the Crow 604
have always admired. A scout on horseback leads the way, 614
deciding the path the dancers will take. During and after the 625
dance, the Crow give gifts to one another. 633

The Crow Indian Fair and Rodeo lasts just a week. But in 645
that short time, the Crow and other Indian people make lasting 656
friendships. They feel their families grow close together. They 665
keep their customs alive—until the next year. 673

William Penn: Father of Pennsylvania

by Zach Cantrell

2
5
8
20
31
41
52
64
74
77
87
100
111
121
132
140
145
156
166
177
189
200
208

William Penn was born in England in 1644 and was the son of a naval officer named Admiral Sir William Penn. As a university student in England in 1660, the younger Penn had trouble adjusting to the religious rule of the university. He left school to travel and study in other countries. After two years of travel, Penn's father sent him to study law in London.

Move to America

King Charles II owed Penn's father a debt. As repayment, the King set up a colony in America for the younger Penn. In 1681, a charter gave William the territory west of the Delaware River between New York and Maryland. He had ruling power over the land, which he wanted to name "Sylvania." The King's council added "Penn." The new colony's name became *Pennsylvania*, which means "Penn's Woods."

In 1682, William Penn, his family, and his followers began a new life in America. Penn and the other colonists were Quakers. They believed that all people had the right to religious freedom to worship as they pleased. In the same year, he signed his first treaty with the Native Americans. In 1684 after the colony was well established, Penn returned to England.

His Later Years

Penn returned to America in 1699. Penn granted a new
constitution for Pennsylvania, which created a one-house
elected assembly. In 1701, however, Penn returned to England
because the English government was trying to place the colony
under its control. While in England, Penn unfortunately
suffered a stroke in 1712, which left him paralyzed until his
death in 1718. His wife, Hannah, and the colonial secretary
James Logan handled Penn's affairs in Pennsylvania. His family
continued owning the colony of Pennsylvania until it gained
statehood during the Revolutionary War.

The Wisdom of Portia

retold from *The Merchant of Venice* by William Shakespeare

by Barbara Anders

4

13

16

Antonio's best friend, Bassanio, wanted to marry Portia, a
woman as wise as she was beautiful and rich. He asked
Antonio for a loan. But Antonio's ships were all at sea. He had
no cash to lend his friend until his ships returned and he sold
their cargo.

Antonio tried to borrow money from Shylock for his friend.
Shylock hated Antonio for taking business away from him. He
saw a chance to get even, and he loaned Antonio the money.
But he made one condition. If Antonio had not paid the loan
back in three months, he must allow Shylock to cut a pound of
flesh from his body. Antonio's ships were due back in port
within a month, so he agreed. He should have no trouble
repaying the loan.

Unfortunately, Antonio's ships
were lost in a storm. The three
months passed, and he couldn't
repay Shylock. Eagerly, Shylock
took Antonio before the Duke to
collect his payment.

Bassanio, now married to
Portia, tried to save his friend.

"I'll pay you three times the
amount of the loan if you'll release
Antonio from his bond. There is no
excuse for such cruelty," Bassanio
told Shylock.

"I need no excuse," snarled
Shylock. "It is the law, and I will
have my payment."

The Duke himself pleaded for
Shylock's mercy. Still, the man
refused.

"I am sorry, my friend," said the
Duke to Antonio. "I have done
everything I can. The law is the law.
But listen. I'm told that a great
lawyer has just arrived. Surely, he
will find a way to stop this."

25
36
49
62
64
74
84
96
108
121
132
143
146
149
156
161
165
171
174
178
184
190
197
204
209
211
216
224
227
232
237
238
245
251
259
266
272
279

Dressed in the hat and robes of a lawyer, Portia entered and 291
stood before the Duke. Portia knew what Antonio had done for 302
her husband. She had arranged a little trickery of her own. 313
Lowering her voice to sound like a man, she said that a great 326
judge had sent her. No one recognized her, not even Bassanio. 337

Studying the agreement, Portia asked, "Did you make this 346
agreement, Antonio?" He admitted he did. 352

"Then Shylock must be merciful." 357

"And why must I?" Shylock demanded. 363

Portia explained that mercy is a great virtue. "It honors both 374
the one who gives it and the one who receives it." 385

Just as before, Shylock wouldn't listen. Portia repeated 393
Bassanio's offer to repay three times the amount of the debt. 404
Still, Shylock demanded his revenge. 409

"Then I am very much afraid, my friends, that the agreement 420
must stand. Prepare, Shylock, to take the pound of flesh from 431
Antonio." 432

Shylock was delighted. "You are a most wise and learned 442
judge," he told Portia. 446

As he prepared his knife, Portia questioned Shylock. "Have 455
you brought a doctor to tend Antonio's wounds?" 463

"There is nothing about that in the agreement," said 472
Shylock. 473

"Yes," agreed Portia, smiling now. "We must obey the 482
agreement to the letter. Therefore, be sure that you do not take 494
one ounce of flesh more or less than a pound. Oh, and the 507
agreement says nothing about blood. You must not spill even 517
one drop of blood. If you do, your life and all your possessions 530
will belong to the Duke. That is the law." 539

Shylock now understood the risk he would be taking to 549
collect the debt. "On second thought, give me triple the amount 560
of the loan as you offered. This isn't worth the trouble." 571

"No!" said Portia. "You refused that in front of the court. Do 583
you now refuse the pound of flesh? You wanted only what the 595
agreement states. Do you now refuse that as well?" 604

Unwilling to risk his life and possessions, the evil Shylock 614
left in disgust. Thanks to Portia's wisdom, Shylock was 623
punished for his greed and cruelty. He got nothing! 632

The Third Doll

by David Downard

3

6

16
26
37
46
47
58
69
80
92
93
103
114
128
141
153
164
168

Sarah roamed about the woods near her new home in Plymouth Colony. Her family had arrived on the ship, *Mayflower*, just one week earlier. She was still adjusting to her new surroundings. Plymouth was so different from her hometown in England.

Suddenly Sarah heard a noise that sounded like a voice. She saw a Native American boy about her own age appear from behind a tall mound of dirt. He approached Sarah and spoke a few words aloud to her, but Sarah could not understand his language.

Sarah noticed that the boy was holding something in his hand. When the boy came nearer, she realized he was holding a doll of some kind. The boy sat down on the ground and held out the doll to Sarah. She joined him on the ground and took the doll. It was crafted from a whole dried apple! Apple seeds had been inserted for the doll's eyes, mouth, and ears. How cleverly it was made!

Quickly, Sarah arose and ran to her house. She returned a   179
minute later, proudly holding a doll of her own. She handed it   191
to the boy, who clearly enjoyed how it looked. Sarah's doll had   203
been made from an old white sock with a small amount of   215
cotton stuffing inside. Sarah had painted the face to look like   226
a clown.   228

Without speaking a word, Sarah and the Native American   237
boy played together with the dolls and had a good time. After a   250
while, Sarah ran back to her house and returned shortly with   261
another sock, which was not yet painted. The boy immediately   271
produced another dried apple from the bag he carried. This one   282
had not yet been made into a doll.   290

Together in silence, Sarah and the boy began to make a   301
third doll. They placed the sock over the apple. Then they   312
designed the face with paint and apple seeds. It was different   323
from the other dolls, but still very nice. After an hour the doll   336
was complete, and Sarah knew she had found her first new   347
friend in Plymouth.   350

A Queen Is Crowned

by Pat Fridell

4

7

How do you become a queen? For Ida Guillory, it took time, practice, and her brother's accordion.

Ida was born in 1929 in Louisiana. Her family lived on a farm. They made their own clothes. They raised chickens and ducks. They hauled water from the well.

It wasn't all hard work. They had fun, too. Uncles and friends would sit on the porch playing harmonicas, accordions, and violins. Ida would crank up her sister's windup record player to listen to records. On Saturdays, the whole family would go to the *fais-dodo* (fā dō do'), a party with music and dancing.

Ida's family moved to a bigger farm in Texas when she was in second grade. They still went to parties. The Louisiana-born neighbors got together to eat Louisiana food and dance to zydeco (zī' də kō') music. Zydeco music is a mixture of Cajun French, African-American, and Hispanic music. It has syncopated rhythms and fast tempos. It's played with accordion, fiddle, bass, saxophone, drums, guitar, and rub-board. A rub-board looks like an old washboard.

19
24
36
46
53
64
73
83
93
104
106
118
129
139
149
157
165
173
181

© Jon Sievert/Michael OCHS ARCHIVE/Venice, CA

When Ida was eighteen years old, her father moved the 191
family to California. One day, her mother brought home an 201
accordion for Ida's brothers. She said, "I want you to keep the 213
music alive, keep it going." 218

Ida didn't even think about playing this accordion. Girls 227
weren't allowed to play. At that time, the accordion wasn't 237
considered a "ladylike" instrument. 241

Ida watched her brother play the accordion. She whispered 250
to herself, "I can do that." But she tried it only when no one 264
could hear her. 267

The accordion was still in the closet when Ida got married. 278
She visited her mother one day and found it. She picked it up 291
and tried a few melodies. Her mom said, "Not bad! You're doing 303
pretty well." 305

Ida played for her parents. She never played anywhere else. 315
Women in her family didn't play music in public. Her dad would 327
say to friends, "You should hear Ida play." But they never did. 339

Motherhood didn't keep her from practicing the accordion. 347
Ida thought she sounded terrible as a beginning accordionist. 356
When she would play a wrong note, she'd hear a groan of "Uh- 369
oh, Mom!" if her children were home. Ida found it easier to 381
practice when she was alone. Then there was no one to say, 393
"That doesn't sound good." 397

One day, her brother urged her to sit in with a band. "Play 410
the song you were playing the other night at home," he said. 422

"Are you crazy?" Ida said. She still thought it wasn't 432
"ladylike" to play the accordion in public. 439

Eventually, she agreed to play at a small party. She thought 450
that the people at the party wanted her to play because they 462
had never seen a woman play the accordion. 472

Soon after that, a band asked her to play with them at a 483
dance. When the evening ended, the bandleader introduced all 492
the musicians. When he got to Ida, he said, "Tonight we're 503
going to crown you Ida: Queen of the Zydeco Accordion and 514
Queen of Zydeco Music." Ida laughed with everyone else. 523

Two weeks later, Ida saw her picture in a San Francisco 534
newspaper. There was an article about her. The reporter called 544
her "Queen Ida." 547

Queen Ida's music career was nonstop after that. Many 556
people wanted her to play for them. She and her band made a 569
record. They toured Europe, Asia, and Africa. In 1982, she 579
received a Grammy award for Best Ethnic/Folk Recording 588
Album. It was the Queen's crowning glory! 595

Worksheets

Common and Proper Nouns

Nouns name people, places, and things. *Proper* nouns name a specific person, place, or thing. Underline the common nouns and circle the proper nouns in each sentence.

1. (Sammy) was born in (Kentucky.)

2. When he was just a <u>puppy</u>, his <u>family</u> moved to (Ohio.)

3. On his <u>way</u> to his new <u>home</u>, (Sammy) became lost.

4. (Martha Green) found him and took him to a <u>kennel</u>.

5. This kind <u>woman</u> finds new <u>homes</u> for lost <u>dogs</u>.

Concrete and Abstract Nouns

If you can touch it, smell it, see it, hear it, or feel it, it's a *concrete* noun. If it's a quality, thought, or idea, it's an *abstract* noun.

In the space at the end of each sentence, write *abstract* or *concrete* to describe the noun underlined in each sentence.

1. The blue <u>car</u> won. _____ **concrete** _____

2. Where is my <u>water</u>? _____ **concrete** _____

3. His <u>dreams</u> are always vivid. _____ **abstract** _____

4. The colonists fought for <u>independence</u>. _____ **abstract** _____

5. That <u>ice cream</u> is extremely cold. _____ **concrete** _____

6. What a great <u>idea</u>! _____ **abstract** _____

UNIT 1 Risks and Consequences • **Lesson 1** *Mrs. Frisby and the Crow*

Common and Proper Nouns

Write either *common* or *proper* in the space next to each noun.

1. cat __**common**__   6. lions __**common**__

2. city __**common**__   7. Boston __**proper**__

3. Canada __**proper**__   8. country __**common**__

4. Earth __**proper**__   9. planet __**common**__

5. daughter __**common**__   10. Sara __**proper**__

Concrete and Abstract Nouns

Write either *abstract* or *concrete* next to each noun.

1. deer __**concrete**__   6. map __**concrete**__

2. school __**concrete**__   7. justice __**abstract**__

3. honesty __**abstract**__   8. chair __**concrete**__

4. love __**abstract**__   9. courtesy __**abstract**__

5. fish __**concrete**__   10. smell __**concrete**__

Nouns

Complete each sentence with a noun from the following list.

work	boxes	Guatemala	city	concerns	farm
beans	life	job	buses	name	

1. Mateo is a worker on a coffee bean **farm**.

2. He walks to get to **work**.

3. His job is to pick ripe **beans**.

4. His brother's **name** is Juan.

5. Juan lives in a busy **city**.

6. Juan takes two **buses** to get to work.

7. His job is to load **boxes** onto trucks.

8. Juan wants Mateo to live with him in **Guatemala** City, Guatemala.

9. Mateo has some **concerns** about living in the city.

10. He is worried about finding a **job**.

11. Mateo knows his **life** will change if he goes to live with his brother.

Write other nouns from the sentences on the blanks.

Mateo _____

Juan _____

brother _____

worker _____

trucks _____

UNIT I   Risks and Consequences • **Lesson 2** *Toto*

Plural Noun

Write the plural form of each of the nouns in the space provided.

1. signal _____ **signals** _____   6. sky _____ **skies** _____

2. brush _____ **brushes** _____   7. planet _____ **planets** _____

3. moose _____ **moose** _____   8. berry _____ **berries** _____

4. movie _____ **movies** _____   9. tooth _____ **teeth** _____

5. glass _____ **glasses** _____   10. city _____ **cities** _____

Possessive Nouns

Write the possessive form in the space provided.

Example: the feathers of a bird   *bird's feathers*

1. the cafeteria of the school   **school's cafeteria**

2. the hands of children   **children's hands**

3. the books of a library   **library's books**

4. the nests that belong to the birds   **birds' nests**

5. the mayor of the city   **city's mayor**

6. the gills of a fish   **fish's gills**

7. the leaves of a plant   **plant's leaves**

8. the legs of frogs   **frogs' legs**

Plural Nouns

Make the sentences below plural by writing the plural form of the underlined nouns. Then read them aloud to your partner.

1. The <u>leaf</u> __**leaves**__ have been raked into <u>pile</u> __**piles**__ and are ready to be put into <u>bag</u> __**bags**__.

2. The <u>dog</u> __**dogs**__ used their <u>tooth</u> __**teeth**__ to bite the ice off their <u>paw</u> __**paws**__.

3. Many <u>child</u> __**children**__ asked their <u>parent</u> __**parents**__ to take them to the space <u>movie</u> __**movies**__.

4. The <u>branch</u> __**branches**__ of the <u>tree</u> __**trees**__ were blowing in the <u>breeze</u> __**breezes**__.

5. The <u>animal</u> __**animals**__ were kept in <u>cage</u> __**cages**__.

Possessive Nouns

Read the story and insert apostrophes in the possessive nouns.

Margaret's family immigrated to America in 1903. They left Glasgow's harbor and arrived at New York's dock a week later. There the captain's assistants directed the passengers into a big building on Ellis Island. In the great hall, the city's immigration officers inspected all the passengers' suitcases. Then, the new arrivals were sent to the doctors' examining rooms.

Organizing and Developing Ideas

Writers often make notes. In the spaces below, list key words or phrases to help you organize and develop your ideas about the story you are going to write.

Answers will vary.

_____

_____

_____

_____

A graphic organizer can help you arrange your ideas. Organize your list of words or phrases into the web below. In the large circle, fill in the main idea of your story. Then, other related thoughts or ideas can go in the smaller circles.

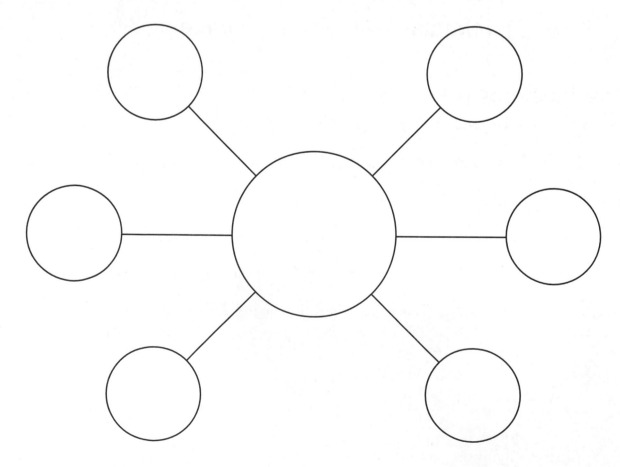

Pronouns

Read the following sentences. Write the noun or nouns that each underlined pronoun stands for.

1. When Martha saw the ugly green sky and dark clouds, <u>she</u> knew a tornado might be heading their way.

Martha

2. Pigs don't roll in mud because <u>they</u> like to be dirty.

Pigs

3. An electronic instrument is one that uses electricity to produce sound. <u>It</u> can't produce sound by itself.

electronic instrument

4. Sandra Day O'Connor was the first woman on the Supreme Court. At age fifty-one, she was also <u>its</u> youngest member.

Supreme Court

5. My sister and I lent our favorite video to our cousin two weeks ago. <u>We</u> want it back.

My sister and I

6. The group ran into trouble when a wall of ice blocked <u>them</u>.

group

7. The teacher read the name from the brown sack that <u>she</u> dangled in the air.

teacher

8. "See?" Todd said. "What did <u>I</u> tell you?"

Todd

Pronouns

Circle the pronouns as you read the story. Write each pronoun from the sentences and the nouns that they refer to.

(1) Birds use (their) voices to communicate. (2) Each male bird picks

out a tree to be (his) territory. (3) Then (he) sings to warn other birds away.

(4) If another bird wants to compete for the same tree, (he) sings too. (5) A

bird wins the tree if (he) sings the loudest. (6) Crows use different cries to

send messages to (their) flock. (7) (They) sing with a high pitch to warn. (8) A

hen tells (her) chicks to run from a dangerous situation. (9) (She) gives a harsh

scream if a hawk is circling overhead. (10) (She) makes a sound like "cut-cut-

cut" if an enemy is on the ground.

1. Pronoun: **their**

    Referent: **birds**

2. Pronoun: **his**

    Referent: **bird**

3. Pronoun: **he**

    Referent: **bird**

4. Pronoun: **he**

    Referent: **another bird**

5. Pronoun: **he**

    Referent: **bird**

6. Pronoun: **their**

    Referent: **crows**

7. Pronoun: **they**

    Referent: **crows**

8. Pronoun: **her**

    Referent: **hen**

9. Pronoun: **she**

    Referent: **hen**

10. Pronoun: **she**

    Referent: **hen**

Topic Sentences

A topic sentence states the main idea of a paragraph. All the other sentences in the paragraph relate to the topic sentence. In each of the following paragraphs, underline the topic sentence.

The stable manager or stable owner has the job of caring for many horses. A stable owner probably owns some horses and also keeps horses for other people. He or she spends a lot of money for feed, fences, and stall repairs. The owners and managers learn all about horse illnesses. They must know which they can handle themselves and which need a veterinarian's help.

One of the most populated areas in the United States is an island. Manhattan is an island that is part of New York City. Almost one-and-a-half million people live in Manhattan's twenty-three square miles.

Pearls are formed by oysters, which are sea animals with two shells. An oyster will make a pearl around anything that gets inside its shell and bothers it. Unlike the minerals and gems that we mine to use in jewelry, pearls come from the sea.

On lined paper, write a paragraph about your favorite book. Underline your topic sentence, and make sure all the sentences in your paragraph relate to your topic sentence.

UNIT I Risks and Consequences • **Lesson 4** *Escape*

Verbs

Underline the verbs in each sentence below. Look for action, linking, and helping verbs. Then tell which kind each verb is.

1. Bill smiled at his son. _____ **smiled, action** _____

2. Joy has taken her sister to the park every Saturday this month. _____
has, helping; taken, action _____

3. I was very sad when you returned home. _____ **was, linking;** _____
returned, action _____

4. Playing tennis is fun. _____ **is, linking (playing is a gerund)** _____

5. The chair is soft and comfortable. _____ **is, linking** _____

_____

6. My cat jumped up onto the table. _____ **jumped, action** _____

_____

7. In Florida, we went sailing. _____ **went, action** _____

8. We made a chocolate cake for your birthday. _____ **made, action** _____

_____

9. My aunt placed the quilt on the bed. _____ **placed; action** _____

_____

10. I enjoyed the movie. _____ **enjoyed, action** _____

11. She is watching her weight. _____ **is, linking; watching, action** _____

12. Sally has been getting headaches lately. _____ **has, helping** _____
been, helping; getting, action _____

UNIT 1   Risks and Consequences • **Lesson 4** *Escape*

Verbs

When you read the following paragraphs, circle the verbs in each sentence. Then above the circle, write whether the verbs in each sentence are action, linking, or helping.

 LV   **HV HV**
   Puppetry (is) an old, respected art in Japan. The Japanese (have) (been)
 AV   **LV**
(performing) with puppets since the 1600s. Their puppets (are) very different
                                                              LV
from puppets of the Western world. Japanese puppets (are) very heavy and
                                                          AV
weigh about 50 pounds each. It takes three people to (work) one puppet. The
                       AV
first person (works) the puppet's head and right hand. A second person
 AV   **AV**
(controls) the puppet's left hand. A third person (runs) the legs.

            LV
   Amelia Earhart (was) a very famous pilot in the 1920s and 1930s. On
             AV   **AV**   **HV LV**
June 1, 1937, she (started) (to fly) around the world. By July 2, she (had) (gone)
             HV   **AV**
22,000 miles and (was) (starting) the last part of her trip. Early that morning,
          AV
she (took off) for tiny Howland Island in the South Pacific Ocean. After that,
       LV   **AV**
she (was) never (heard) from again.

UNIT 1   Risks and Consequences • **Lesson 4** *Escape*

Graphic Organizer—Web

A web is a graphic organizer that can help you develop and organize
your ideas. In the large circle, write an important goal you wish to
pursue. Then in the smaller circles write the necessary steps that
may be involved in attaining your goal.

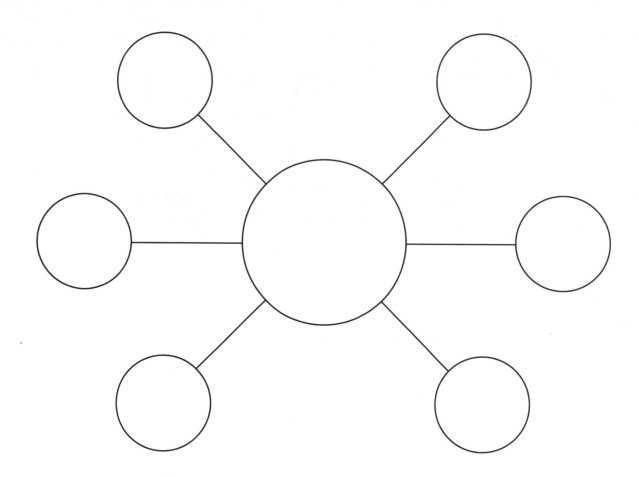

UNIT I   Risks and Consequences • **Lesson 5** *Mae Jemison: Space Scientist*

What Is a Sentence?

Read the following sentences, and circle the subject and underline
the predicate in each sentence.

1. (My mother) is a good cook.

2. (The bald eagle) is the national bird of the United States.

3. (The sun) sets in the west.

4. (The crashing sound of the waves) lulled me to sleep.

5. (The store) will open at 10 a.m.

6. (The ball) rolled into the pond.

7. (Marcia) spoke to her friend on the telephone for an hour.

8. (The dark blue sky) is filled with twinkling stars.

9. (Tina) was thirsty.

10. (I) can hear wolves howling at night.

UNIT I   **Risks and Consequences** • **Lesson 5** *Mae Jemison: Space Scientist*

What Is a Sentence?

Read the story. Then on the lines below, copy the story. Circle the subject and underline the predicate in each sentence.

(Thomas Alva Edison) was a great inventor. (He) improved many things created by other inventors. (One of his best known inventions) is the telegraph. (It) is still used today. (People) use the telegraph to send important messages.

(Edison's passion) led him to combine some of his own inventions. (He) combined his three favorite inventions in 1915. (These inventions) were the light bulb, the sound-recording device, and the motion picture projector. (He) produced the first motion picture with sound with these inventions.

    Thomas Alva Edison was a great inventor. He improved many things created by other inventors. One of his best-known inventions is the telegraph. It is still used today. People use the telegraph to send important messages.

    Edison's passion led him to combine some of his own inventions. He combined his three favorite inventions in 1915. These inventions were the light bulb, the sound-recording device, and the motion picture projector. He produced the first motion picture with sound with these inventions.

UNIT I   Risks and Consequences • **Lesson 6** *Two Tickets to Freedom*

Kinds of Sentences

**Read each of the sentences, and insert the appropriate end
punctuation in the space provided. Then, in the space provided,
identify the sentence as either declarative, exclamatory,
interrogative, or imperative.**

1. Do not cross the street **.** __imperative__

2. We are leaving for the beach now **.** __declarative__

3. What time is it **?** __interrogative__

4. I will never sell my bicycle to you **!** __exclamatory__

5. Get me a towel **.** __imperative__

6. Are you coming to my party on Friday night **?** __interrogative__

7. They will help you with your homework **.** __declarative__

8. I forgot to buy milk at the supermarket **.** __declarative__

9. Why were you late for the concert **?** __interrogative__

10. Take out the trash **.** __imperative__

UNIT I Risks and Consequences • **Lesson 6** *Two Tickets to Freedom*

Kinds of Sentences

Read the stories below, and circle each end mark that is incorrect. Write the correct end mark above the circle. Then, in the space provided, identify each sentence as either declarative, exclamatory, interrogative, or imperative.

1.   I wonder what is the meaning of the expression, "Nothing ventured, nothing

gained." ___**declarative**___ I think there are two possible meanings for this

expression. ___**declarative**___ The expression can possibly mean that taking

adventures is beneficial. ___**declarative**___ It can also mean that if "I don't try to

do something, I can't achieve it!" ___**exclamatory**___ Is this saying about adventures

or about taking risks? ___**interrogative**___ What do you think?

___**interrogative**___

2.   "Hey! Wait for me!" ___**exclamatory**___ yelled Danny. "Where are you going?"

___**interrogative**___

"We are going to see the monkeys," Matt answered. ___**declarative**___

"I want to go with you," said Danny. ___**declarative**___

"Okay, come on!" ___**exclamatory**___

Revising

The purpose of revising is to make sure your writing expresses your ideas clearly and completely. Reevaluate the content of your writing using the following questions. Select a piece of writing and check off the questions below as you revise your paper.

Paragraphs

❏ Does each sentence relate to your topic sentence?

❏ Does each sentence connect smoothly with the next?

Sentences

❏ Do the sentences read smoothly?

❏ Have I combined sentences that were too short?

❏ Have I broken sentences that were too long into two shorter sentences?

❏ Have I varied the beginnings of the sentences?

Words

❏ Have I changed words that were repeated too often?

❏ Do transition words connect ideas?

UNIT I   Risks and Consequences • **Lesson 7** *Daedalus and Icarus*

Review

Read the following sentences, and write an (n) over the nouns, a (p) over pronouns, (av) over action verbs, (hv) over helping verbs, and (lv) over linking verbs. Then circle the subject and underline the predicate. In the space provided, identify the type of sentence.

         N   AV   N   P N
1. (The bird) gathered twigs for his nest. ___**declarative**___

         AV N
2. (you) Stop talking. ___**imperative**___

    P NLV   N
3. (Our car) is dented from the accident. ___**declarative**___

   P HV   AV   N   N
4. (I) will never finish this report by Monday! ___**exclamatory**___

           N   LV   AV   N
5. (The local bookstore) is sponsoring a book fair. ___**declarative**___

   HV P AV   P   N
6. Will (you) come with me to the store? ___**interrogatory**___

Write the plural form of the following nouns on the line.

1. story _____**stories**_____   6. dress _____**dresses**_____

2. house _____**houses**_____   7. sheep _____**sheep**_____

3. mouse _____**mice**_____   8. life _____**lives**_____

4. scarf _____**scarves**_____   9. dog _____**dogs**_____

5. party _____**parties**_____   10. shrimp _____**shrimp**_____

UNIT I   Risks and Consequences • **Lesson 7** *Daedalus and Icarus*

Review

Read the following sentences. Underline the pronoun and circle the noun the pronoun refers to in each sentence.

1. The (members) of the committee argued among <u>themselves</u>.

2. (Gabriel) spent three hours washing and waxing <u>his</u> car.

3. (Nathan) played baseball until dusk, when <u>he</u> suddenly remembered <u>he</u> was supposed to meet <u>his</u> brother at the library.

4. (Sharon) has packed for <u>her</u> vacation.

5. The (cashier) left <u>his</u> cash register open.

Write a helping verb to complete each sentence.

1. Helen _____**went**_____ shopping this afternoon.

2. My mother won't see a movie until she _____**has**_____ read a review of it.

3. The birthday party _____**is**_____ going to be a surprise.

4. It _____**has**_____ been sunny for the past three days.

5. My friend _____**is**_____ moving to a new house tomorrow.

UNIT 2 Dollars and Sense • **Lesson 1** *Starting a Business*

Types of Sentences

Underline each independent clause in the following compound sentences. Circle each conjunction.

1. She knew she had to hurry, (but) she was tired and could barely walk.

2. Morgan rowed harder, (and) soon he saw the shore.

3. We will have to stop for something to eat, (or) I will collapse.

4. The actor read the script, (and) the story impressed him.

5. It was a rainy, dreary day, (yet) Linda was very cheerful.

6. The sun was very strong and hot, (and) we were very thirsty after our long walk.

Read each complex sentence below. Underline each dependent clause. Circle the conjunction that begins that clause.

1. (After) the class sang the song, the little boy repeated it to himself.

2. (Since) we are not going out to dinner, I have to start cooking.

3. Many insects and animals stay alive in the pond all winter (though) the temperature drops below freezing.

4. You need to leave for your appointment early (because) the weather is bad.

5. (When) it is cold outside, I like to read by the fireplace.

6. Come to dinner on Friday (if) you're free.

UNIT 2   Dollars and Sense • **Lesson I** *Starting a Business*

Types of Sentences

Read the paragraph below, and identify each type of sentence as simple, compound, or complex.

(1) Sam went to the circus. (2) While he was there, he saw a group of people doing tricks on bicycles. (3) Some of them were sitting on the handlebars, and some of them were riding backwards. (4) The performers made it look very easy. (5) They also seemed to enjoy what they were doing.

(6) After the performance, Sam talked to the people who did the tricks on bicycles. (7) He asked how they learned to do the tricks. (8) The performers said they often fell off when trying new tricks, but they had gear to keep them from getting hurt.

1. **simple** _____
2. **complex** _____
3. **compound** _____
4. **simple** _____
5. **simple** _____
6. **complex** _____
7. **simple** _____
8. **compound** _____

UNIT 2 Dollars and Sense • **Lesson 2** *Henry Wells and William G. Fargo*

Capitalization

Read each of the following items, and correct any errors in capitalization.

1. dr. Michael Santori

   Dr. Michael Santori

2. *Charlotte's web*

   Charlotte's Web

3. Chicago, Illinois

   correct

4. Metropolitan museum of art

   Metropolitan Museum of Art

5. North of Bakersfield

   north of Bakersfield

6. March 2, 1999

   correct

7. tuesdays and Saturdays

   Tuesdays and Saturdays

8. The supreme court

   The Supreme Court

9. The midwest

   The Midwest

10. 111 Main Street, Roanoke, Virginia

    correct

UNIT 2 Dollars and Sense • **Lesson 2** *Henry Wells and William G. Fargo*

Capitalization

Read the following paragraph, and correct any errors in capitalization. Rewrite each sentence in the space provided.

1) From the time john was Ten, he knew he wanted to help people get along. 2) When other kids were fighting on the School Playground, he would help break up the fights. 3) Then, He would talk to the kids about why they had been hurting each other. 4)Today, John is twenty-five years old, and he works at a Middle School in springview, illinois. 5) He is a conflict moderator. 6) when students have trouble getting along, he helps them work out their problems without fighting.

1. **capitalize John, lowercase ten** _____

   _____

2. **lowercase school playground** _____

   _____

3. **lowercase he** _____

   _____

4. **lowercase middle school, capitalize**

   springview, illinois _____

5. **correct** _____

   _____

6. **capitalize when** _____

   _____

Name _____ Date _____

UNIT 2 Dollars and Sense • **Lesson 3** *Elias Sifuentes, Restaurateur*

Periods and End Punctuation

Read the following paragraphs, and correct errors in end punctuation and the use of periods.

1. The Aztecs were good farmers? They grew corn, tomatoes, beans, cotton, and potatoes. They ate thin corn pancakes. Mexicans still eat this pancake, and they call it a tortilla! You may have eaten one yourself.

   The Aztecs were good farmers. They grew

   corn, tomatoes, beans, cotton, and potatoes.

   They ate thin corn pancakes. Mexicans still eat

   this pancake, and they call it a tortilla. You may

   have eaten one yourself!

2. Imagine driving a car whose engine makes no noise. Imagine driving a car in which you never have to check the oil or fill the gas tank. You just need to put the car in the sun for a couple of hours? An engine that makes no noise. Never check the oil or gas! Fill it up with sun? That's right. This new kind of car is solar-powered.

   Imagine driving a car whose engine makes no

   noise. Imagine driving a car in which you never

   have to check the oil or fill the gas tank. You

   just need to put the car in the sun for a couple

   of hours. An engine that makes no noise?

   Never check the oil or gas? Fill it up with sun?

   That's right! This new kind of car is solar-

   powered.

Worksheet 24   UNIT 2 • Lesson 3   Intervention

Periods and End Punctuation

Read the following paragraphs, and rewrite the sentences, correcting end punctuation and use of periods.

1. Will you call me today. I have something to tell you, and it is urgent. I would really like it if we could speak! You must call me soon.

   Will you call me today? I have something to tell you, and it is urgent. I would really like it if we could speak. You must call me soon!

2. Jonas Salk discovered a way to control polio? Have you heard of this great doctor. He became famous in 1955. He received many honors for his work. His vaccine was in the form of a shot!

   Jonas Salk discovered a way to control polio. Have you heard of this great doctor? He became famous in 1955. He received many honors for his work. His vaccine was in the form of a shot.

3. Guion (Guy) Stewart Bluford, Jr, was born on November 22, 1942, in Philadelphia. How did Guy Bluford become an expert in the world of space science! His father was an engineer who also invented things. His mother was a teacher! The Blufords encouraged Guion and his two younger brothers to work hard and to reach for success?

   Guion (Guy) Stewart Bluford, Jr., was born on November 22, 1942, in Philadelphia. How did Guy Bluford become an expert in the world of space science? His father was an engineer who also invented things. His mother was a teacher. The Blufords encouraged Guion and his two younger brothers to work hard and to reach for success.

UNIT 2 Dollars and Sense • **Lesson 4** *Food from the 'Hood: A Garden of Hope*

Commas

Remember that commas are used in dates, addresses, parts
of a letter, or direct address. Read each sentence. Place an arrow
where commas belong. Then write the sentences correctly on the
lines below.

1. Karen started her business on May 31 1996.

   Karen started her business on May 31, 1996.

   _____

2. It was started in Denver Colorado.

   It was started in Denver, Colorado.

   _____

3. Karen what do you sell?

   Karen, what do you sell?

4. Dear Ben

   Dear Ben,

   _____

5. Starting July 1 2002 I will have a sale on quilts

   Starting July 1, 2002, I will have a sale on

   quilts.

   _____

6. Sincerely Ellen

   Sincerely, Ellen

   _____

7. Hey Mom may I eat the leftover pizza?

   Hey, Mom, may I eat the leftover pizza?

   _____

UNIT 2   Dollars and Sense • **Lesson 4** *Food from the 'Hood: A Garden of Hope*

Commas

Read the story and add commas where they belong. Write the story correctly on the lines below.

Benjamin heard that a group of slaves planned to escape. Joshua‸Ruth‸and Caleb planned to travel the Underground Railroad that night. Benjamin wanted to go. He needed to know what time they would be leaving and from where.

Joshua said, "Just listen for the song over yonder‸Benjamin."

Benjamin sat‸listened‸and waited. Soon‸he heard a faraway melody drifting from the fields. Benjamin heard the promise of freedom‸happiness‸and joy in that song. He met Joshua‸Ruth‸and Caleb in the field. They were ready for the long‸hard‸and dangerous journey on the Underground Railroad.

Benjamin heard that a group of slaves planned to escape. Joshua, Ruth, and Caleb planned to travel the Underground Railroad that night. Benjamin wanted to go. He needed to know what time they would be leaving and from where.

Joshua said, "Just listen for the song over yonder, Benjamin."

Benjamin sat, listened, and waited. Soon, he heard a faraway melody drifting from the fields. Benjamin heard the promise of freedom, happiness, and joy in that song. He met Joshua, Ruth, and Caleb in the field. They were ready for the long, hard, and dangerous journey on the Underground Railroad.

Name _____ Date _____

Quotation Marks and Underlining

Read each of the following passages. Correct the errors in quotation marks and underlining.

1. Mimi gushed "I can't wait to see the Compact Discs in concert"!

   Mimi gushed, "I can't wait to see the Compact Discs in concert!"

2. "I am tired of knocking on doors," Chuck said.

   correct

3. Grandfather sat on the porch, rocking to and fro in his squeaky old chair, "Did I ever tell you about the winter of thirty-three?" "It was the winter of the big freeze." "The temperature had dropped to sixty degrees below zero."

   Grandfather sat on the porch, rocking to and fro in his squeaky old chair. "Did I ever tell you about the winter of thirty-three? It was the winter of the big freeze. The temperature had dropped to sixty degrees below zero."

4. Roy Donaldson is my favorite author, Matt said. "his new short story, The Frog Who Couldn't Ribbit, is my favorite story."

   "Roy Donaldson is my favorite author," Matt said. "His new short story, The Frog Who Couldn't Ribbit, is my favorite story."

Quotation Marks and Underlining

Read the following paragraph. Rewrite the paragraph, correcting errors in quotation marks and underlining.

"Children, I've got terrible news" started Mom. Our television is broken.

I felt my knees buckle. My sister gasped and put her hands over her face. My brothers were too horrified to move. When we overcame the shock, we all started talking.

"Mom, you must be fooling," said Tim.

"Mom, call someone who can fix it." "Do something!" yelled Stu.

"Now I do not want anyone to lose control," said Mom in her calmest voice. I feel that this will be a new opportunity for you to go outdoors or read something and improve your minds.

That was six weeks ago, and we have not had time for television since!

"Children, I've got terrible news," started Mom. "Our television is broken."

I felt my knees buckle. My sister gasped and put her hands over her face. My brothers were too horrified to move. When we overcame the shock, we all started talking.

"Mom, you must be fooling," said Tim.

"Mom, call someone who can fix it. Do something!" yelled Stu.

"Now I do not want anyone to lose control," said Mom in her calmest voice. "I feel that this will be a new opportunity for you to go outdoors or read something and improve your minds."

That was six weeks ago, and we have not had time for television since!

Colons, Semicolons, and Other Marks

Read the following paragraph, and correct any errors in the use of colons, semicolons, dashes, hyphens, and parentheses. Rewrite the paragraph correctly in the space provided.

Christian has a beat:up golf cart. He uses the cart—to drive to the beach. The beach is only two blocks from his house, but Christian needs the cart to carry his beach supplies; chairs, towels, a cooler, and an umbrella. He likes the golf cart better because it is easy to park: He just pulls it up on the grass (and unloads his things.)

Christian has a beat-up golf cart. He uses the cart to drive to the beach. The beach is only two blocks from his house, but Christian needs the cart to carry his beach supplies: chairs, towels, a cooler, and an umbrella. He likes the golf cart better because it is easy to park; he just pulls it up on the grass and unloads his things.

_____

_____

_____

_____

_____

_____

_____

Colons, Semicolons, and Other Marks

Add colons, semicolons, and other marks to the following sentences.

1. Julie's flight arrived at exactly 2 19 p.m. yesterday afternoon.

   Julie's flight arrived at exactly 2:19 p.m. yesterday

   afternoon.

2. Miami—a popular city for tourists—lies on Biscayne Bay.

   correct

3. Jackie checked the contents of the bag; flashlight, extra batteries, jacket, cap, and first aid kit.

   Jackie checked the contents of the bag: flashlight,

   extra batteries, jacket, cap, and first aid kit.

4. The mule is a strong animal: it is also very stubborn.

   The mule is a strong animal; it is also very stubborn.

Write one sentence that contains a colon, one that contains a hyphen, and one that contains a dash.

Colon

Answers will vary.

_____

Hyphen

Answers will vary.

_____

Dash

Answers will vary.

_____

Name _____ Date _____

Review

Read the story. Circle the subject, and underline the predicate in each sentence. Then, identify each sentence as simple, compound, or complex.

(Many insects) touch and smell to communicate. __**simple**__

(They) use their antennae to send and receive information. __**simple**__

(The main job of scout ants) is to search for food, and (they) go back to the nest after they find food. __**compound**__ (They) leave a scented trail behind. __**simple**__ (Other ants) follow the scent trail to find food and bring it back to the nest. __**simple**__ As the ants return to the nest, (they) release more scent in order to preserve the trail. __**complex**__

(The ant that gets the last piece of food) leaves no scent trail on his way back to the nest. __**simple**__ By not leaving a scent trail, (he) is sending the message that there is no more food. __**complex**__

Review

Read the story, and add commas where they belong.

Benjamin heard that a group of slaves planned to escape. Joshua, Ruth, and Caleb planned to travel the Underground Railroad that night. Benjamin wanted to go. He needed to know what time they would be leaving and from where.

Joshua said, "Just listen for the song over yonder, Benjamin."

Benjamin sat, listened, and waited. Soon, he heard a faraway melody drifting from the fields. Benjamin heard the promise of freedom, happiness, and joy in that song. He met Joshua, Ruth, and Caleb in the field. They were ready for the long, hard, and dangerous journey on the Underground Railroad.

Read the story, and insert quotation marks where they are needed.

"Grandpop, I wish you would let me help you," said Roy.

"I don't need any help," said the old man. His gruff voice turned into a wheeze. "I am going to have tea. Will you join me?"

Roy pulled up a chair and sat down. Grandpop stared at him.

"So they let a boy like you become a doctor?" he asked.

Roy laughed. "Well, you might say that. Now, Grandpop, I just need to listen to your lungs." Roy started opening his black bag.

"Put those toys away," said Grandpop. "I think our water is boiling We will drink our tea and then we can go for a walk."

"Let's just do one thing at a time," said Roy.

"That is good advice, doctor," grinned Grandpop.

Apostrophes—Possessive Nouns and Contractions

Read the story and circle each possessive noun and contraction that is incorrect. Write the possessive or contraction correctly above the circle. Then write the story correctly on the lines below.

don't
Lisa knows that people (dont) always have to talk to communicate.
mother's
She knows that when her (mothers) head moves from left to right it always

means "no."

everybody's
Lisa thought that (everybodys) behavior was the same all over the
isn't
world. However, she found out that it (isnt) the same. For example, people in
don't
Japan (dont) shake hands. They bow to say hello or good-bye.
Lisa's
(Lisas) conclusion is that body language can communicate different

things in different cultures.

Lisa knows that people don't always have to talk to

communicate. She knows that when her mother's head

moves from left to right it always means "no."

Lisa thought that everybody's behavior was the

same all over the world. However, she found out that it

isn't the same. For example, people in Japan don't

shake hands. They bow to say hello or good-bye.

Lisa's conclusion is that body language can

communicate different things in different cultures.

_____

_____

Apostrophes—Possessive Nouns and Contractions

Read the story and circle each possessive noun and contraction that is incorrect. Write the possessive or contraction correctly above the circle. Then write the story correctly on the lines below.

women's
In colonial times, (womens) lives were much different than they are

Abigail's
today. (Abigails) daughter, Elizabeth, was about to get married. She was

trained in the skills of housekeeping.

Elizabeth's
(Elizabeths) dowry was made by her own hands. She spun and wove her

mother's   didn't
own linens. She used her (mothers) spinning wheel, because she (didnt) have

one of her own yet.

wasn't
Housekeeping (wasnt) the only chore women had to do. They also had

to work in the fields. They helped to clear land and plant crops right

Women's   weren't
alongside their husbands. (Womens) lives (werent) easy.

In colonial times, women's lives were much different

than they are today. Abigail's daughter, Elizabeth, was

about to get married. She was trained in the skills of

housekeeping.

Elizabeth's dowry was made by her own hands. She

spun and wove her own linens. She used her mother's

spinning wheel, because she didn't have one of her

own yet.

Housekeeping wasn't the only chore women had to

do. They also had to work in the fields. They helped to

clear land and plant crops right alongside their

husbands. Women's lives weren't easy.

Apostrophes—Possessive Nouns and Contractions

Read the paragraph, and underline words that contain errors in the use of apostrophes. Then in the space provided, rewrite the paragraph and correct the errors.

Today, people do'nt need to be nervous about having operations. Hospital's make sure that their operating rooms and tools are clean. They know that you can'nt be too careful when it comes to germs. Doctor's and nurse's wear masks, gloves, and special clothes to keep germs away from the patient. They've learned that a patients' chances of healing are better in a clean setting.

Today, people don't need to be nervous about having operations. Hospitals make sure that their operating rooms and tools are clean. They know that you can't be too careful when it comes to germs. Doctors and nurses wear masks, gloves, and special clothes to keep germs away from the patient. They've learned that a patient's chances of healing are better in a clean setting.

_____

_____

_____

_____

_____

Verb Tenses

Read the following sentences and circle the verbs with the incorrect tense. Write the verb correctly over the circle. Then copy the sentences correctly on the lines below.

finished

1. Christina (finish) all her home work yesterday.

   ## Christina finished all her home work yesterday.

will eat

2. I (am eating) dinner in fifteen minutes.

   ## I will eat dinner in fifteen minutes.

is

3. Right now, Eric (was) playing soccer.

   ## Right now, Eric is playing soccer.

4. Ali read a book last night.

   ## Ali read a book last night.

shopped

5. I (shops) with Brent last week.

   ## I shopped with Brent last week.

is

6. It is night, so everyone (are) sleeping.

   ## It is night, so everyone is sleeping.

joined

7. Jay (join) the club in second grade.

   ## Jay joined the club in second grade.

will

8. Next month, we (were) travel to Oregon.

   ## Next month, we will travel to Oregon.

UNIT 3   From Mystery to Medicine • **Lesson 2** *Sewed Up His Heart*

Verb Tenses

Read the following sentences and circle the verbs with the incorrect
tense. Write the verb correctly over the circle. Then copy the
sentences correctly on the lines below.

1. Riley and Ben (were) play baseball next weekend.

   will

   <u>Riley and Ben will play baseball next weekend.</u>

2. The new puppies (are) born last week.

   were

   <u>The new puppies were born last week.</u>

3. Mica's mother (was) on the phone right now.

   is

   <u>Mica's mother is on the phone right now.</u>

4. Next year, my brother (is) turn five.

   will

   <u>Next year, my brother will turn five.</u>

5. Yesterday I (pick) a blue flower.

   picked

   <u>Yesterday I picked a blue flower.</u>

6. People were standing in line all day.

   <u>People were standing in line all day.</u>

7. Jonathan always (am) very quiet.

   is/was

   <u>Jonathan always is (was) very quiet.</u>

8. Harry, my pet cat, (find) a dead mouse yesterday.

   found

   <u>Harry, my pet cat, found a dead mouse yesterday.</u>

Subject-Verb Agreement

Read the story and circle the verbs that are incorrect. Write the correct verb above the circle. Then write the story correctly on the lines below.

       is   **is**   **wants**

The sky (are) gray and cloudy. The lake (are) choppy. Mike (want) to go

                      asks   **am**

sailing this afternoon. He (ask) me to go with him. I (is) afraid because of the

                   are

weather. Many people (is) docking their boats already.

     jumps   **helps**   **sail**

Mike (jump) in the boat. He (help) me into the boat. We (sails) for only a

                                    is

few minutes before big, black clouds roll in. The rain (are) coming down fast

      has   **are**

and hard. Mike (have) trouble keeping the boat afloat. I keep thinking we (is)

      uses   **is**

going to drown. Mike (use) the radio to call for help. Soon, our call (are)

                              rescue

answered by the Coast Guard. They (rescues) us just in time.

    The sky is gray and cloudy. The lake is choppy. Mike wants to go sailing this afternoon. He asks me to go with him. I am afraid because of the weather. Many people are docking their boats already.

    Mike jumps in the boat. He helps me into the boat. We sail for only a few minutes before big, black clouds roll in. The rain is coming down fast and hard. Mike has trouble keeping the boat afloat. I keep thinking we are going to drown. Mike uses the radio to call for help. Soon, our call is answered by the Coast Guard. They rescue us just in time.

Subject-Verb Agreement

Read the story and circle the verbs that are incorrect. Write the correct verb above the circle. Then write the story correctly on the lines below.

chase   **track**
Many people (chases) tornadoes. Many people (tracks) tornadoes to
follow
gather scientific data. Others (follows) tornadoes for adventure. Peter Porter
follows   **travels**
is a scientist. He (follow) tornadoes for adventure and work. He usually (travel)
                                                                      gets
to Kansas, Oklahoma, and Texas during tornado season. Sometimes he (get)
watches   **knows**
close to them. Often, he (watch) them from a distance. He (know) that
                                        says
following tornadoes is dangerous. But Pete (say) his work tests his

survival skills.

   Many people chase tornadoes. Many people track

tornadoes to gather scientific data. Others follow

tornadoes for adventure. Peter Porter is a scientist. He

follows tornadoes for adventure and work. He usually

travels to Kansas, Oklahoma, and Texas during

tornado season. Sometimes he gets close to them.

Often, he watches them from a distance. He knows

that following tornadoes is dangerous. But Pete says

his work tests his survival skills.

_____

_____

_____

Subject-Verb Agreement

Read the paragraph. Then in the space provided, rewrite the paragraph and correct the errors in subject/verb agreement.

Jane and John makes lunch for the picnic. Jeff packs a ball, and Bob

bring mitts. Joan tell everyone to bring their bathing suits. Sam wash some

cups. Karen and Jim looks for a first-aid kit.

**Jane and John make lunch for the picnic. Jeff packs**

**a ball, and Bob brings mitts. Joan tells everyone to**

**bring their bathing suits. Sam washes some cups.**

**Karen and Jim look for a first-aid kit.**

_____

_____

_____

_____

_____

_____

_____

_____

_____

Name _____ Date _____

Pronoun/Antecedent Agreement

Read the following sentences and circle the pronouns. Then write the pronouns on the lines below and write the word or words that are the pronouns' antecedents.

1. After school, Maria and Mimi were hungry, so (they) had a snack.

2. The puppy chased (its) tail.

3. The ball player threw down (his) bat.

4. Mr. Hansen claimed math was (his) favorite subject to teach.

5. The lion and (his) mate were looking for shelter.

6. Beth gave (her) dog a bath on Saturday.

they	Maria and Mimi
its	puppy
his	player
his	Mr. Hansen
his	lion
her	Beth

Name _____ Date _____

Pronoun/Antecedent Agreement

Read the following sentences and circle the pronouns. Then write the pronouns on the lines below and write the word or words that are the pronouns' antecedents.

1. "Betsy, (you) are so smart!" exclaimed Ms. Rose.

2. Everyone thought (their) painting was the best.

3. Kris liked to help (his) father work on the car.

4. Karen and I like chocolate sauce on (our) ice cream.

5. At the zoo, the giraffe plays with (her) baby.

6. Becky's book had (its) cover torn off.

7. The football players wore (their) new uniforms.

8. Some people think (they) know everything!

you	Betsy
their	Everyone
his	Kris
our	Karen and I
her	giraffe
its	book
their	players
they	people

UNIT 3 From Mystery to Medicine • **Lesson 5** *The New Doctor*

Pronouns

Read the story and decide on the correct pronoun for each blank space. Write the word on the line. Then write the story correctly on the lines below.

Natalie broke ____**her**____ arm when ____**she**____ fell off ____**her**____ bike. ____**Her**____ mother took ____**her**____ to the hospital. ____**She**____ was in a lot of pain. At the hospital, they gave her some medicine to help the pain, and ____**they**____ took X-rays of ____**her**____ arm. The doctor saw that ____**it**____ was broken. ____**He/She**____ put her arm in a cast to allow the bones to heal. A few weeks later, the doctor took another X-ray of Natalie's arm. ____**He/She**____ said ____**it**____ was as good as new.

____**Natalie broke her arm when she fell off her bike. Her mother took her to the hospital. She was in a lot of pain. At the hospital, they gave her some medicine to help the pain, and they took X-rays of her arm. The doctor saw that it was broken. She (He) put her arm in a cast to allow the bones to heal. A few weeks later, the doctor took another X-ray of Natalie's arm. She (He) said it was as good as new.**____

_____

_____

_____

Name _____   **Date** _____

Pronouns

Read the story and decide on the correct pronoun for each blank space. Write the word on the line. Then write the story correctly on the lines below.

Kelly is going on a camping trip with **her** family. **They** plan to go into the mountains. **Her** brother Dan likes to hike. Kelly likes canoeing. So does **her** sister. Dad has a broken arm, so **he** is going to float in the creek and read.

Most days the family will cook **their** food over a campfire. Kelly's sister, Angie, likes to fish. So, **she** will try to catch fish each morning. Once or twice, the family will go to a lodge for dinner. Dan's happy about that because **he** has a hard time cooking pizza on a campfire. **His** favorite campfire food is marshmallows.

Kelly is going on a camping trip with her family. They plan to go into the mountains. Her brother Dan likes to hike. Kelly likes canoeing. So does her sister. Dad has a broken arm, so he is going to float in the creek and read.

Most days the family will cook their food over a campfire. Kelly's sister, Angie, likes to fish. So, she will try to catch fish each morning. Once or twice, the family will go to a lodge for dinner. Dan's happy about that because he has a hard time cooking pizza on a campfire. His favorite campfire food is marshmallows.

Name _____ Date _____

Adjectives

Read the story and complete each sentence with an adjective from the following list. Write the word in the blank. Then write the story correctly on the lines below.

white   soaring   new   bright   three   green   pretty

Seth painted __three__ pictures for his mother's birthday. He couldn't decide which he liked best. The first picture was of a beautiful, __green__ tree. The second picture showed a lovely, __white__ seagull flying in the sky. Seth's third painting was of __bright__, yellow sunflowers growing in a park. Which __pretty__ painting would be perfect for his mother? Suddenly, Seth knew the answer! He would paint a __new__ picture showing all three: a large tree, a __soaring__ seagull, and sunny flowers.

___Seth painted three pictures for his mother's birthday. He couldn't decide which he liked best. The first picture was of a beautiful, green tree. The second picture showed a lovely, white seagull flying in the sky. Seth's third painting was of bright, yellow sunflowers growing in a park. Which pretty painting would be perfect for his mother? Suddenly, Seth knew the answer! He would paint a new picture showing all three: a large tree, a soaring seagull, and sunny flowers.___

Name _____ Date _____

Adjectives

Read the story and complete each sentence with an adjective from the following list. Write the word in the blank. Then write the story correctly on the lines below.

blowing   winter   800   dog   overjoyed   two   deep   brave

In Nome, Alaska, __winter__ snow was fierce. The only way to get around was by __dog__ sled. A very __brave__ dog named Balto led a dog-sled team that carried food and tools.

One day, __two__ children became ill. They needed medicine or they would die. Medicine they needed was put on a train __800__ miles away. But the snowstorm was awful. The train could not get through the __deep__, __blowing__ snow. Dogs had to haul the medicine.

Balto was ready. Balto ran on until he finally arrived in Nome. The __overjoyed__ people were safe.

__In Nome, Alaska, winter snow was fierce. The only__
__way to get around was by dog sled. A very brave dog__
__named Balto led a dog-sled team that carried food__
__and tools.__

__One day, two children became ill. They needed__
__medicine or they would die. Medicine they needed was__
__put on a train 800 miles away. But the snowstorm was__
__awful. The train could not get through the deep,__
__blowing snow. Dogs had to haul the medicine.__

__Balto was ready. Balto ran on until he finally arrived__
__in Nome. The overjoyed people were safe.__

UNIT 3 From Mystery to Medicine • **Lesson 6** *The Story of Susan La Flesche Picotte*

Adjectives

Read the paragraph, and insert adjectives in the spaces.

Papa's store was usually **Answers will vary.** and

crowded on Saturday mornings. I put on my **Answers will vary.** ,

blue jacket and Mama and I walked to the store to help Papa. Papa is a

baker and makes **Answers will vary.** bread. I saw Papa's

Answers will vary. face when we walked in the door. He was

always happy to have his family working with him. Someday I want to own a

bakery like Papa.

Explain what information each adjective in the above paragraph
provides about the noun that it describes. How do the adjectives
help readers understand and enjoy the paragraph?

Answers will vary. _____

_____

_____

_____

_____

_____

_____

_____

_____

UNIT 3   From Mystery to Medicine • **Lesson 6** *The Story of Susan*
                                                        La Flesche Picotte

Adjectives

Write a short paragraph about a place you like to visit, using
adjectives to make your writing clearer and more interesting.

Answers will vary. _____

_____

_____

_____

_____

_____

_____

_____

_____

_____

_____

_____

_____

_____

_____

_____

_____

Adverbs

Read the following sentences and circle the adverbs. Write another adverb that could be used in the sentence above the circle. Then copy the sentences with the new adverbs on the lines below.

Answers will vary.

1. The puppy whimpered (quietly) for its mother.

The puppy whimpered _____ for its mother.

2. Kate sang (joyfully.)

Kate sang _____ .

3. The hikers were (hopelessly) lost.

The hikers were _____ lost.

4. The gentle rain (softly) fell.

The gentle rain _____ fell.

5. The coyotes were (wildly) barking.

The coyotes were _____ barking.

6. Police had the house (completely) surrounded.

Police had the house _____ surrounded.

UNIT 3   From Mystery to Medicine • **Lesson 7** *Shadow of a Bull*

Adverbs

Read the following sentences and circle the adverbs. Write another adverb that could be used in the sentence above the circle. Then copy the sentences with the new adverbs on the lines below.
  Answers will vary.

1. Becca (neatly) wrote her name on the board.

   Becca _____ wrote her name on the board.

2. The frogs (noisily) croaked in the pond.

   The frogs _____ croaked in the pond.

3. James smiled (brightly) for the photographer.

   James smiled _____ for the photographer.

4. The biker (nearly) crashed into me.

   The biker _____ crashed into me.

5. At hearing Mr. Jett's voice, the class was quiet (instantly.)

   At hearing Mr. Jett's voice, the class was _____

   quiet _____ .

6. Lisa looked (shyly) at Aaron.

   Lisa looked _____ at Aaron.

7. The orchestra (happily) played a Bach concerto.

   The orchestra _____ played a Bach concerto.

8. Scott and Andrew (naturally) looked alike.

   Scott and Andrew _____ looked alike.

UNIT 3 From Mystery to Medicine • **Lesson 7** *Shadow of a Bull*

Adverbs

Read the story and circle the adverbs that are incorrect. Write the correct word above the circle. Then write the story correctly on the lines below.

Ira takes long vacations. His two dogs are very big and he cannot ~~easy~~ **easily**
~~kind~~ **kindly** travel with them. His mother ~~kind~~ took care of them in the past, but she
recently ~~recent~~ moved to another state. He is **anxiously** ~~anxious~~ searching for a place to leave

his dogs so he can visit his mother.

He heard about an animal boarding business that is part of a veterinary
carefully **freely** clinic. The dogs are ~~careful~~ examined when they arrive. The dogs run ~~free~~ in
generally an open yard twice daily to get exercise. The clinic ~~general~~ provides good

and fresh water.

    Ira takes long vacations. His two dogs are very big
and he cannot easily travel with them. His mother
kindly took care of them in the past, but she recently
moved to another state. He is anxiously searching for a
place to leave his dogs so he can visit his mother.

    He heard about an animal boarding business that is
part of a veterinary clinic. The dogs are carefully
examined when they arrive. The dogs run freely in an
open yard twice daily to get exercise. The clinic
generally provides good and fresh water.

Comparative and Superlative Adjectives

**Read the story and circle the correct adjective in each sentence.
Then write the story correctly on the lines below.**

This afternoon was (hottest (hotter)) than yesterday. But Kim, Megan,

and I still wanted to cross the desert in our old truck. We were in the middle

of the desert when our truck started sputtering. We needed water for the

truck, but we also needed water to drink. I was the (thirstier (thirstiest)) of

all. We had to decide whether water for the truck was ((more important) most

important) than water to drink.

While we were fixing the truck, Megan screamed. The (larger (largest))

lizard I'd ever seen was staring at us. We worked ((faster) fastest). Soon, we

were able to restart the truck and leave the desert.

**This afternoon was hotter than yesterday. But Kim,
Megan, and I still wanted to cross the desert in our old
truck. We were in the middle of the desert when our
truck started sputtering. We needed water for the
truck, but we also needed water to drink. I was the
thirstiest of all. We had to decide whether water for the
truck was more important than water to drink.**

**While we were fixing the truck, Megan screamed.
The largest lizard I'd ever seen was staring at us. We
worked faster. Soon, we were able to restart the truck
and leave the desert.**

UNIT 4 Survival • **Lesson I** *Island of the Blue Dolphins*

Comparative and Superlative Adjectives

Write the comparative and superlative forms of each word below.

1. quick _____ quicker _____ quickest

2. important _____ more important _____ most important

3. slowly _____ more slowly _____ most slowly

4. soon _____ sooner _____ soonest

5. hard _____ harder _____ hardest

6. pretty _____ prettier _____ prettiest

7. interesting _____ more interesting _____ most interesting

8. happy _____ happier _____ happiest

9. small _____ smaller _____ smallest

10. great _____ greater _____ greatest

Comparative and Superlative Adjectives

Read the story and circle the correct adjective in each sentence. Then write the story correctly on the lines below.

During the seventeenth century, American colonial furniture was of the (simpler, (simplest)) sort. The settlers brought only the (more, (most)) important goods from Europe. They had to make new furniture when they got to America. Because the settlers had little furniture, clothing hung on pegs along the wall.

Some years later, the colonists' businesses grew ((stronger,) strongest) and they had more money to spend. They were able to build ((bigger,) biggest) houses. They got more furniture and had the (nicer, (nicest)) cabinets to store their clothing.

During the seventeenth century, American colonial furniture was of the simplest sort. The settlers brought only the most important goods from Europe. They had to make new furniture when they got to America. Because the settlers had little furniture, clothing hung on pegs along the wall.

Some years later, the colonists' businesses grew stronger and they had more money to spend. They were able to build bigger houses. They got more furniture and had the nicest cabinets to store their clothing.

UNIT 4 Survival • **Lesson 2** *Arctic Explorer: The Story of Matthew Henson*

Adverbs

Read each of the following sentences and circle the incorrect
adverbs. Write the correct adverb above the circle. Then write the
sentences correctly on the lines below.

happily
1. I will (happy) drive you to the store.

   I will happily drive you to the store. _____

   cheerfully
2. Father (cheerful) frosted the cake.

   Father cheerfully frosted the cake. _____

   easily
3. The players won the big game (easy)

   The players won the big game easily. _____

   really
4. The jokes were (real) funny.

   The jokes were really funny. _____

   quietly
5. Peter tiptoed in the room (quiet)

   Peter tiptoed in the room quietly. _____

6. Jonathan rapidly ran to the corner.

   Jonathan rapidly ran to the corner. _____

   carefully
7. Sarah (careful) put the china away.

   Sarah carefully put the china away. _____

   hopelessly
8. Mother looked at the broken glass (hopeless)

   Mother looked at the broken glass hopelessly. _____

9. The choir sang joyously.

   The choir sang joyously. _____

   wildly
10. Everyone was (wild) dancing around the room.

    Everyone was wildly dancing around the room. _____

Adverbs

**Read each of the following sentences and circle the incorrect
adverbs. Write the correct adverb above the circle. Then write the
sentences correctly on the lines below.**

slowly
1. Jordan (slow) boarded down the mountain.

   Jordan slowly boarded down the mountain.

   powerfully
2. The tiger's jaws were (powerful) strong.

   The tiger's jaws were powerfully strong.

   terribly
3. Luke knew he drew (terrible.)

   Luke knew he drew terribly.

   quickly
4. The kittens (quick) ran toward their mother.

   The kittens quickly ran toward their mother.

   loudly
5. The musician pounded (loud) on his drum.

   The musician pounded loudly on his drum.

6. Art swam swiftly through the lake.

   Art swam swiftly through the lake.

   smoothly
7. This car drives (smooth.)

   This car drives smoothly.

   warmly
8. Father smiled (warm) at the little baby.

   Father smiled warmly at the little baby.

   slowly
9. The snails moved (slow) down the sidewalk.

   The snails moved slowly down the sidewalk.

10. Jenna scored perfectly on the test.

   Jenna scored perfectly on the test.

UNIT 4   Survival • **Lesson 3** *McBroom and the Big Wind*

Conjunctions

Read the story. Use the conjunctions from the list to complete each sentence. Write the story correctly on the lines below.

and   but   or

Gloria Estefan, a Latino pop singer, was in a bad accident. Her bus slid

on ice, ___**and**___ it crashed on the highway. She broke her back in the

accident. Gloria had two choices: she could give up any hope of singing

again, ___**or**___ she could work hard to get her strength back. Gloria did

not know whether she would fully recover, ___**but**___ she was not about to

give up. Music played an important part in her recovery, ___**and**___ she was

back on stage one year after the accident. Gloria Estefan was grateful to her

fans, ___**and**___ she expressed her thanks through music.

___**Gloria Estefan, a Latino pop singer, was in a bad**___

accident. Her bus slid on ice, and it crashed on the

highway. She broke her back in the accident. Gloria

had two choices: she could give up any hope of

singing again, or she could work hard to get her

strength back. Gloria did not know whether she would

fully recover, but she was not about to give up. Music

played an important part in her recovery, and she was

back on stage one year after the accident. Gloria

Estefan was grateful to her fans, and she expressed

her thanks through music.

UNIT 4   Survival • **Lesson 3** *McBroom and the Big Wind*

Conjunctions

Read the story. Use the conjunctions from the list to complete each sentence. Write the story correctly on the lines below.

and   but   or

At high tide, Lori stood near the cliffs. The sounds of powerful waves **and**

howling wind were all around her. She felt frightened. If the storm passed over the island,

what would happen to her house? Would it be torn down **or** damaged by the wind?

Dad said they would be safer on higher ground, **and** the sea would not be

able to surround them there. Lori hoped her dad was right, **but** she was not so sure.

That night the wind grew louder **and** louder. Rain came down in buckets. Lori

pulled her blanket around her. Her parents were there, **but** Lori was scared.

_____**At high tide, Lori stood near the cliffs. The sounds**_____
_____**of powerful waves and howling wind were all around**_____
_____**her. She felt frightened. If the storm passed over the**_____
_____**island, what would happen to her house? Would it be**_____
_____**torn down or damaged by the wind?**_____
_____**Dad said they would be safer on higher ground, and**_____
_____**the sea would not be able to surround them there. Lori**_____
_____**hoped her dad was right, but she was not so sure.**_____
_____**That night, the wind grew louder and louder. Rain**_____
_____**came down in buckets. Lori pulled her blanket around**_____
_____**her. Her parents were there, but Lori was scared.**_____

_____

_____

Conjunctions

Read the following paragraph. Insert the words and or but when a
conjunction is necessary to correct a sentence. Rewrite the
paragraph on the lines below, including any necessary conjunctions.

The old man hoped to thank the girl she was gone. He told her story to

others. The summer sun was warm the corn grew tall. In autumn the corn

was harvested the people had a feast.

**The old man hoped to thank the girl, but she was
gone. He told her story to others. The summer sun was
warm, and the corn grew tall. In autumn the corn was
harvested, and the people had a feast.**

UNIT 4 Survival • **Lesson 4** *The Big Wave*

Prepositions

Read the story and complete each sentence with a preposition from the following list. Write the preposition in the blank. Then write the story correctly on the lines below.

about   in   for   on   during   with   in

Women worked hard __during__ the Civil War. These women grew

vegetables and herbs __in__ their gardens. The herbs were used

__in__ medicines. Because there were few doctors, the women learned

__about__ healing with herbs.

Many families did not have much money. They often reused old faded

clothes. Women took the clothes apart __with__ scissors. Then, they

sewed the clothes back together using the inside material __for__ the

outside. Finally, they added new cuffs and collars __on__ the clothes.

__Women worked hard during the Civil War. These__

__women grew vegetables and herbs in their gardens.__

__The herbs were used in medicines. Because there__

__were few doctors, the women learned about healing__

__with herbs.__

__Many families did not have much money. They often__

__reused old faded clothes. Women took the clothes__

__apart with scissors. Then, they sewed the clothes back__

__together using the inside material for the outside.__

__Finally, they added new cuffs and collars on the__

__clothes.__

UNIT 4 Survival • **Lesson 4** *The Big Wave*

Prepositions

Read the story and complete each sentence with a preposition from the following list. Write the preposition in the blank. Then write the story correctly on the lines below.

by with in to from about on of

Sam likes to read **about** cowboys. He finds many stories

in books and magazines.

Sam often walks **to** the library. Mrs. Green shows him copies

of old movie posters. The librarian has watched most of these old

cowboy pictures again and again. She shares her favorites **with** Sam.

Sam's room is filled with things **from** the Old West. He has a

small stagecoach and a photo signed **by** Roy Rogers **on**

his shelves.

_____Sam likes to read about cowboys. He finds many_____

stories in books and magazines._____

_____Sam often walks to the library. Mrs. Green shows_____

him copies of old movie posters. The librarian has_____

watched most of these old cowboy pictures again and_____

again. She shares her favorites with Sam._____

_____Sam's room is filled with things from the Old West._____

He has a small stagecoach and a photo signed by Roy_____

Rogers on his shelves._____

_____

UNIT 4   Survival • **Lesson 4** *The Big Wave*

Prepositions

Read the following paragraph. Insert prepositions where they are needed. Then rewrite the paragraph on the lines below, including the necessary prepositions.

Pretzels were first baked Italian monks. They twisted the dough loops.

The twists looked like a pair folded arms. They looked like a child's arms

folded prayer. The monks gave out the pretzels as a reward. Pretzels were

invented that very moment!

Pretzels were first baked by Italian monks. They twisted the dough into loops. The twists looked like a pair of folded arms. They looked like a child's arms folded in prayer. The monks gave out the pretzels as a reward. Pretzels were invented at that very moment!

_____

_____

_____

_____

_____

_____

_____

_____

UNIT 4   Survival • **Lesson 5** *Anne Frank: Diary of a Young Girl*

Contractions

Read the following sentences. Write the contraction for the underlined words above them. Then write the sentences with the contractions on the lines below.

wouldn't
1. Marybeth <u>would not</u> go into the haunted house.

Marybeth wouldn't go into the haunted house.

I'll
2. <u>I will</u> not be going to the mall on Saturday.

I'll not be going to the mall on Saturday.

he'd
3. Mike said that <u>he would</u> be coming over soon.

Mike said that he'd be coming over soon.

aren't
4. We <u>are not</u> stopping at the park today.

We aren't stopping at the park today.

couldn't
5. The puppy <u>could not</u> jump over the fence.

The puppy couldn't jump over the fence.

They're
6. <u>They are</u> tired from mowing the lawn.

They're tired from mowing the lawn.

we're
7. My mom said <u>we are</u> coming over soon.

My mom said we're coming over soon.

didn't
8. I <u>did not</u> want to go to sleep so early.

I didn't want to go to sleep so early.

They'll
9. Hurry up! <u>They will</u> be here soon.

Hurry up! They'll be here soon.

can't
10. Mike <u>cannot</u> stand to play football.

Mike can't stand to play football.

UNIT 4   Survival • **Lesson 5** *Anne Frank: Diary of a Young Girl*

Contractions

Read the following sentences. Write the contraction for the underlined words above them. Then write the sentences with the contractions on the lines below.

isn't
1. That book <u>is not</u> yours.

That book isn't yours. _____

won't
2. Molly's shirt <u>will not</u> fit me.

Molly's shirt won't fit me. _____

Who's
3. <u>Who is</u> going to go on the field trip?

Who's going to go on the field trip? _____

They're
4. <u>They are</u> in Ms. Sinclair's music class.

They're in Ms. Sinclair's music class. _____

haven't
5. I <u>have not</u> ever been to France.

I haven't ever been to France. _____

It's
6. <u>It is</u> often rainy in March.

It's often rainy in March. _____

You'll
7. <u>You will</u> like my brother, Bruce.

You'll like my brother, Bruce. _____

she'd
8. Everyone thought <u>she would</u> win the election.

Everyone thought she'd win the election. _____

wasn't
9. The puppy <u>was not</u> house broken yet.

The puppy wasn't house broken yet. _____

I'm
10. <u>I am</u> very anxious to see the movie.

I'm very anxious to see the movie. _____

Adjectives and Adverbs

Read the story. Underline the adverbs, list them, and write down the verb they modify. Circle the adjectives, list them, and write down the noun they modify.

Andrew was a soldier who <u>bravely</u> fought in the Vietnam War. He was a (young) man when he fought in the war. The Vietnam War was the (longest) war that the United States took part in. Andrew kept a diary and wrote in it <u>nightly</u>. He wrote about the people in a (large) village in South Vietnam. His job was to protect the people in the village. Andrew wanted to make sure the women, (small) children, and (older) people were safe. He <u>often</u> shared his food with a (little) boy he called "Doc." Doc was Andrew's (best) friend. Both Andrew and Doc wanted the war to end <u>quickly</u>. One day, their wish came true. Andrew and Doc woke up one morning, and the war was over!

Adverbs	Adjectives
bravely—fought	young—man
nightly—wrote	longest—war
often—shared	large—village
quickly—end	small—children
	older—people
	little—boy
	best—friend

Adjectives and Adverbs

Read the story. Underline the adverbs, list them, and write down the verb they modify. Circle the adjectives, list them, and write down the noun they modify.

In 1768, Martha and her girlfriends <u>happily</u> baked (large) pies. The men were building a (wooden) house. (Hard) work was <u>quickly</u> turned into a party.

The (young) women laughed and gossiped. (Long) tables were <u>slowly</u> set up. Everything was ready for the (great) feast. The (good) smell <u>completely</u> distracted the (hungry) men.

The men <u>finally</u> finished the (plain) house. The women <u>kindly</u> served the (simple) food. All of them toasted the house <u>loudly</u> with (rustic) jars of cider.

Adverbs	Adjectives
happily—baked	large—pies
quickly—was turned	wooden—house
slowly—were set	hard—work
completely—distracted	young—women
finally—finished	long—tables
kindly—served	great—feast
loudly—toasted	good—smell
	hungry—men
	plain—house
	simple—food
	rustic—jars

Prepositional Phrases

Read the story, and underline the prepositional phrases. Then list the prepositional phrases on the lines below.

Do you think it would be fun to keep crickets <u>for pets</u>? People <u>in Japan</u> have been doing that <u>for centuries</u>. They claim that crickets keep them cool <u>on summer nights</u>. The whirring <u>of a cricket's wings</u> stirs the air <u>into a breeze</u>.

If somebody can't catch a cricket, they buy one <u>at the market</u>. Crickets are kept <u>inside bamboo or plastic cages</u>. They are fed raw vegetables and bits <u>of bread</u>. A bowl filled <u>with water</u> is important, too.

1. for pets _____
2. in Japan _____
3. for centuries _____
4. on summer nights _____
5. of a cricket's wings _____
6. into a breeze _____
7. at the market _____
8. inside bamboo or plastic cages _____
9. of bread _____
10. with water _____

Prepositional Phrases

Read the story, and underline the prepositional phrases. Then list the prepositional phrases on the lines below.

White tailed deer living <u>in open fields</u> use signals to communicate <u>with each other</u>. The oldest doe <u>among the group</u> is the leader. She flashes the white underside <u>of her tail</u> when she senses danger. The other members <u>of the herd</u> know to run.

Animals <u>with strong family ties</u> mark their territory. Black bears scratch tree trunks to tell other bears <u>about their territory</u>.

Some signals are used to alert other animals. Cats do several things to scare their enemies. They make themselves look larger <u>by raising their fur</u>. They lash their tails back and forth. And they show sharp teeth.

1. <u>**in open fields**</u>
2. <u>**with each other**</u>
3. <u>**among the group**</u>
4. <u>**of her tail**</u>
5. <u>**of the herd**</u>
6. <u>**with strong family ties**</u>
7. <u>**about their territory**</u>
8. <u>**by raising their fur**</u>

Prepositional Phrases

Read the paragraph below, and put brackets around the prepositional phrases. Underline the object of each preposition.

This is a picture [of <u>me</u>] [at my grandma's <u>farm.</u>] Grandma and I feed the

chickens and the sheep [in the <u>barnyard.</u>] Sometimes we walk [to the apple

<u>orchard</u>] and pick some apples [for a <u>pie.</u>] Behind the <u>orchard</u>] is a huge field

[of <u>wildflowers.</u>] I like to pick flowers [for <u>Grandma.</u>]

In "Gwendolyn Brook, Poet," you read about the poet Gwendolyn Brooks. Write a short poem about something that you like to do. Use prepositional phrases in your poem, and underline each prepositional phrase.

_____

_____

_____

_____

_____

_____

_____

_____

_____

_____

_____

UNIT 5 Communication • **Lesson 2** *"We'll Be Right Back After These Messages"*

Clauses

Read the following pairs of independent clauses. Then on the lines below, combine them into one sentence using a comma and a conjunction.

1. Peter bought a used car. He repaired it himself.

   <u>**Peter bought a used car, and he repaired it himself.**</u>

2. Aunt Judy flew here from New York. She would rather have taken the train.

   <u>**Aunt Judy flew here from New York, but she would**</u>
   <u>**rather have taken the train.**</u>

3. I might buy a new green sweater. Maybe I will buy a new jacket.

   <u>**I might buy a new green sweater, or maybe I will buy**</u>
   <u>**a new jacket.**</u>

4. Ginny is practicing the piano. She would rather be watching television.

   <u>**Ginny is practicing the piano, but she would rather**</u>
   <u>**be watching television.**</u>

5. The Bears are in first place. They are going to play the Wolves today.

   <u>**The Bears are in first place, and they are going to**</u>
   <u>**play the Wolves today.**</u>

6. Megan learned first aid. Dan learned to do CPR.

   <u>**Megan learned first aid, and Dan learned to do CPR.**</u>

7. Jamie is very smart. He won the school spelling bee.

   <u>**Jamie is very smart, and he won the school spelling**</u>
   <u>**bee.**</u>

Clauses

Read the following pairs of independent clauses. Then on the lines below, combine them into one sentence using a comma and a conjunction.

1. We can ride the bus to school. We can walk to school.

   We can ride the bus to school, or we can walk.

2. Spinach is very good for you. Some people don't like it.

   Spinach is very good for you, but some people don't like it.

3. It is snowing today. Wear your warmest winter jacket.

   It is snowing today, so wear your warmest winter jacket.

4. Beth liked vanilla ice cream. Sarah preferred chocolate.

   Beth liked vanilla ice cream, but Sarah preferred chocolate.

5. Stephen was the captain of the team. Jamal was the coach.

   Stephen was the captain of the team, and Jamal was the coach.

6. Martin is the best speller in class. Today he didn't do so well.

   Martin is the best speller in class, but today he didn't do so well.

7. It was a beautiful sunny day. It was very cold.

   It was a beautiful sunny day, but it was very cold

Direct Objects

Read the sentences, and circle the direct objects.

1. Max sliced the (pie) into eight pieces.

2. Matthew broke his (arm) while skiing.

3. The flight attendant served (coffee and tea.)

4. My little sister loves chocolate (cake.)

5. Did you find your lost (kitten?)

6. Mom and Dad were going (shopping.)

7. Everyone likes to watch (baseball.)

8. Uncle Rich sold his (bike) to me.

9. Paula gave me her phone (number.)

10. The detective solved the difficult (case.)

11. Jeremy plays (football) for the Titans.

12. Mitch and Mike were cleaning the (kitchen.)

13. I carelessly spilled (milk) on the floor.

14. Can you come to my (house) today?

15. Let's play a (game) after dinner.

UNIT 5 Communication • **Lesson 3** *Breaking Into Print*

Direct Objects

Read the sentences, and circle the direct objects.

1. Tim likes the new Spanish (teacher.)

2. The VCR can record my favorite (show.)

3. Leslie's father drove his (car) to San Diego.

4. Michael was writing a (letter) to Jessie.

5. The attendant will fill the gas (tank.)

6. Bart dropped an (egg) on the floor.

7. Everyone was touched by the sad (movie.)

8. Did you lose another (pair) of socks?

9. Can you call your (Grandmother) today?

10. My mother made my favorite (dessert.)

11. My dad likes (money.)

12. The audience applauded the (actors.)

13. James scored the winning (goal.)

14. The infielder missed that (ball.)

15. I can't understand the (directions.)

Sentence Fragments

Read the following paragraphs and underline the sentences that are not complete. Then copy the paragraph on the lines below, adding words to make the fragments complete sentences.

If you don't use sign language, you might not realize how often you communicate without using words. Did your eyebrows just go up in surprise? <u>That might mean.</u> <u>Smile to let me know you agree, understand, or like my ideas?</u>

<u>High fives and thumbs up are ways of saying.</u> We nod or shake our heads, grin or frown, put both hands on our hips, stomp our feet, and twiddle our thumbs to communicate without using words. <u>When we want the dog.</u> <u>When we forget, when we remember, or when we want to say, "Over here!"</u>

<u>Sentences will vary; however, check to make sure that they are complete sentences.</u>

_____

_____

_____

_____

_____

_____

_____

_____

Sentence Fragments

Read the following paragraphs and underline the sentences that are not complete. Then copy the paragraph on the lines below, adding words to make the fragments complete sentences.

Humans have found a number of ways of communicating with animals. Be trained to come when we whistle, clap, and call. We use hand signals to keep them sitting in one spot. Most cats cannot be bothered to follow commands unless food. Mice will go running all through a maze to find cheese. Teaching tricks to monkeys, elephants, tigers, and seals.

Animals communicate with us, too, but we only recognize a few of their signals. To let us know we had better mind our own business. Animals lick, nuzzle, wag their tails, and hop into our laps to let us know that they like us.

Sentences will vary; however, check to make sure that they are complete sentences.

_____

_____

_____

_____

_____

_____

_____

UNIT 5   Communication • **Lesson 5** *Louis Braille*

Subject/Verb Agreement

Read the story, and circle the incorrect verbs. Write the correct verb
above the circle. Then write the story correctly on the lines below.

          has   **teaches**
The colonial school (have) only one room. Mr. Madison (teach) everybody.
  work   **sit**
Older kids (works) on benches along the wall. Younger kids (sits) on lower

benches in the middle of the room.
             knows   **are**
Mr. Madison (know) math, English, and science. Some lessons (is) learned
                            receives
by the whole school, but each group (receive) special attention.
      make
Students (makes) their own books at home. They write with goose
          boil
quills. The parents (boils) maple bark to make the ink.

    **The colonial school has only one room. Mr. Madison
teaches everybody. Older kids work on benches along
the wall. Younger kids sit on lower benches in the
middle of the room.**

    **Mr. Madison knows math, English, and science.
Some lessons are learned by the whole school, but
each group receives special attention.**

    **Students make their own books at home. They write
with goose quills. The parents boil maple bark to make
the ink.**

_____

_____

_____

UNIT 5 Communication • **Lesson 5** *Louis Braille*

Subject/Verb Agreement

Read the story, and circle the incorrect verbs. Write the correct verb above the circle. Then write the story correctly on the lines below.

When families stepped on board ships leaving for the New World, they ~~was~~ *were*

walking into new lives. Some went seeking freedom to practice their beliefs in their

own ways. Some had committed crimes and ~~was~~ *were* being shipped out of the country

rather than being sent to prison. Some just had a ~~desires~~ *desire* to try their luck in a new land.

Those who had already been to America spoke about its many ~~rich~~ *riches* Opportunities

seemed limitless. On the ship's deck, those brave folks making the crossing ~~looks~~ *looked* out at

more than the sea. They looked out at hopes, dreams, and a new life.

<u>When families stepped on board ships leaving for the New World, they were walking into new lives. Some went seeking freedom to practice their beliefs in their own ways. Some had committed crimes and were being shipped out of the country rather than being sent to prison. Some just had a desire to try their luck in a new land.</u>

<u>Those who had already been to America spoke about its many riches. Opportunities seemed limitless. On the ship's deck, those brave folks making the crossing looked out at more than the sea. They looked out at hopes, dreams, and a new life.</u>

UNIT 5   Communication • **Lesson 6** *My Two Drawings*

Skills Review: Sentence Fragments

Read the following sentences. Write *sentence* on the line next to a complete sentence. Write *fragment* on the line next to a sentence fragment. Then expand the fragments into complete sentences on the lines below.

1. Rides the bus to school everyday. _____fragment_____

2. The girl with the telephone. _____fragment_____

3. My mother baked oatmeal cookies. _____sentence_____

4. Our cat caught a mouse. _____sentence_____

5. Most people. _____fragment_____

6. Makes gifts for all her friends. _____fragment_____

7. My three best friends. _____fragment_____

8. Jennifer struck out. _____sentence_____

9. What did you? _____fragment_____

10. Plays for the Giants. _____fragment_____

Answers will vary.

_____

_____

_____

_____

_____

_____

_____

UNIT 5 Communication • **Lesson 6** *My Two Drawings*

Skills Review: Sentence Fragments

Read the following sentences. Write *sentence* **on the line next to a complete sentence. Write** *fragment* **on the line next to a sentence fragment. Then expand the fragments into complete sentences on the lines below.**

1. The wheat farmer. _____**fragment**_____

2. Donated his home for the party. _____**fragment**_____

3. Aunt Susie made applesauce. _____**sentence**_____

4. The girl with the blonde hair. _____**fragment**_____

5. Five silly puppies. _____**fragment**_____

6. Kyle swam across the lake. _____**sentence**_____

7. Sang in the choir last weekend. _____**fragment**_____

8. Had to visit the dentist. _____**fragment**_____

9. Yesterday morning Rick. _____**fragment**_____

10. The geese flew overhead. _____**sentence**_____

Answers will vary. _____

_____

_____

_____

_____

_____

_____

_____

Review Skill: Parts of Speech—Nouns, Verbs, Adjectives, Adverbs

Read the following sentences. Mark *N* for noun, *V* for verb, *ADJ* for adjective, and *ADV* for adverb. Then write the nouns, verbs, adjectives, and adverbs under the correct headings on the lines below.

   N   V ADJ   N
1. Michelle saw beautiful flowers.

     N V ADJ ADJ N
2. An apple is a delicious, red fruit.

    N V   ADV   N
3. The fans cheered wildly for the team.

   N V ADV ADV   ADJ N
4. Matt skied rapidly down the steep slope.

   N V ADJ ADJ   N
5. Kris liked short, sweet poems.

  ADJ N   V   ADV
6. The old man laughed loudly.

Nouns	Verbs	Adjectives	Adverbs
Michelle	saw	beautiful	wildly
flowers	is	delicious	rapidly
apple	cheered	red	down
fruit	skied	steep	loudly
fans	liked	short	
team	laughed	sweet	
Matt		old	
slope			
Kris			
poems			
man			

Name _____   Date _____

Review Skill: Parts of Speech—Nouns, Verbs, Adjectives, Adverbs

Read the following sentences. Mark *N* for noun, *V* for verb, *ADJ* for adjective, and *ADV* for adverb. Then write the nouns, verbs, adjectives, and adverbs under the correct headings on the lines below.

    N V ADV   N
1. They ran frantically toward the door.
    ADJ N V   N
2. The cautious deer sipped water.
    N   V   ADJ ADJ N
3. Becky heard strange, scary noises.
    N V   N ADV
4. Pete won the game fairly.
    ADJ N   V   ADJ
5. The old dog moved slowly.
    ADJ   N   V ADJ N
6. Twenty children told silly jokes.

Nouns	Verbs	Adjectives	Adverbs
They	ran	cautious	frantically
door	sipped	strange	fairly
deer	heard	scary	slowly
water	won	old	
Becky	moved	Twenty	
noises	told	silly	
Pete			
game			
dog			
children			
jokes			

UNIT 6   A Changing America • **Lesson 1** *Early America*

Review Skill: Parts of Speech

Read the following sentences. Mark *N* for noun, *V* for verb, *ADJ* for adjective, and *ADV* for adverb.

    N   N   V   ADJ   N   ADJ   N

1. James Wilson was an important figure in American history.

    N   V   V   N   V   N

2. Wilson was born in Scotland and then came to America.

      V   ADJ   N   N

3. He started his law practice in Pennsylvania.

    N   V   N   N   V ADJ N

4. Wilson married Rachel Bird, and they had six children.

    N   V   ADJ   ADJ   N

5. Wilson was a great and convincing speaker.

      V   V   N

6. He helped draft the *Constitution*.

UNIT 6 A Changing America • **Lesson 2** *The Voyage of the Mayflower*

Capitalization and Punctuation

Read the story. Circle any word that should begin with a capital
letter and write the word correctly above it. Add any missing end
punctuation. Then write the story correctly on the lines below.

Eileen
      . Her
(eileen) Saxon was a beautiful baby, but she was born with a serious heart problem (her)
     . If
heart did not receive enough oxygen from her lungs (if) she didn't get help, she would die **.**
Dr.
     . A
(dr.) Helen Taussig thought of a way to make Eileen's blood flow better (a) surgeon

operated on Eileen using Dr. Taussig's ideas **.**
Eileen's
(eileen's) surgery was done on November 29, 1945.
At
     . In
(at) first, she hovered between life and death (in) time, she grew stronger and her
     . Thanks
happy parents were able to take her home (thanks) to Dr. Taussig's research, Eileen's life

was saved.

**Eileen Saxon was a beautiful baby, but she was
born with a serious heart problem. Her heart did not
receive enough oxygen from her lungs. If she didn't get
help, she would die.**

**Dr. Helen Taussig thought of a way to make Eileen's
blood flow better. A surgeon operated on Eileen using
Dr. Taussig's ideas.**

Eileen's surgery was done on November 29, 1945.

**At first, she hovered between life and death. In time,
she grew stronger and her happy parents were able to
take her home. Thanks to Dr. Taussig's research,
Eileen's life was saved.**

Capitalization and Punctuation

Read the story. Circle any word that should begin with a capital
letter and write the word correctly above it. Add any missing end
punctuation. Then write the story correctly on the lines below.

Letters
(letters) during colonial times did not have envelopes. A letter was
                                                    Paul Revere
merely folded and had the following type of address: To Mr. (paul revere,)
                Milk Street
near the sign of Plow, in (milk street,) Boston.
Social
(social) life was also different. People used to get together in their
                                              . People
houses because there were no cafes or restaurants (people) who wanted
                          . That
visitors would leave their shutters open (that) way nobody was surprised

when company came.

    Letters during colonial times did not have

envelopes. A letter was merely folded and had the

following type of address: To Mr. Paul Revere, near the

sign of Plow, in Milk Street, Boston.

    Social life was also different. People used to get

together in their houses because there were no cafes

or restaurants. People who wanted visitors would

leave their shutters open. That way nobody was

surprised when company came.

_____

_____

_____

UNIT 6   A Changing America • **Lesson 3** *Pocahontas*

Review Skill: Prepositional Phrases

Read the following sentences. In each sentence, underline the prepositional phrase and circle the preposition. Then write the prepositional phrases on the lines below.

1. There was spilled milk (on) the floor.

   on the floor _____

2. Martha turned her head (toward) me.

   toward me _____

3. Everyone (in) my family loves cherries.

   in my family _____

4. (Under) the roof, the birds built a nest.

   Under the roof _____

5. The painting (of) sunflowers is my favorite.

   of sunflowers _____

6. I found my brush (inside) the drawer.

   inside the drawer _____

7. (Beneath) the sofa, I found my books.

   beneath the sofa _____

8. Jayne studied (before) the exam.

   before the exam _____

9. I bought the frame (for) my parents.

   for my parents _____

10. Your drawing goes (outside) the lines.

    outside the lines _____

UNIT 6 A Changing America • **Lesson 3** *Pocahontas*

Review Skill: Prepositional Phrases

Read the following sentences. In each sentence, underline the prepositional phrases, and circle the prepositions.

1. Ling looked (for) the entry (in) the index.

2. Mark Twain wrote (about) life (across) America.

3. The sun fell (beyond) the horizon.

4. The books (around) the table are mine.

5. The horse jumped (over) the creek.

6. Mario waited (near) the bus stop (for) his ride.

7. Draw a line (under) the nouns.

8. The house (across) the street is vacant.

9. (After) the storm, there was a rainbow.

10. Everybody (in) the class knew the answer.

UNIT 6 A Changing America • **Lesson 4** *Martha Helps the Rebels*

Compound Sentences

Read the following sentences, and put an arrow where the comma should be. Write the correct conjunction for joining the sentences over the arrow. Then copy the compound sentence correctly on the lines below.

1. The English test is tomorrow. **but** I haven't studied yet
   ^

   <u>The English test is tomorrow, but I haven't</u>

   <u>studied yet.</u>

2. Tony finished the race first. **and** He won the blue ribbon.
   ^

   <u>Tony finished the race first, and he won the blue</u>

   <u>ribbon.</u>

3. Eric feeds the fish in the mornings. **and** Leslie feeds them at night.
   ^

   <u>Eric feeds the fish in the mornings, and Leslie feeds</u>

   <u>them at night.</u>

4. The baby crawled to his mom. **and** He smiled up at her.
   ^

   <u>The baby crawled to his mom, and he smiled up</u>

   <u>at her.</u>

5. Are you hungry? **or** Have you eaten lunch?
   ^

   <u>Are you hungry, or have you eaten lunch?</u>

6. Brian plays tennis everyday. **and** He usually wins.
   ^

   <u>Brian plays tennis everyday, and he usually wins.</u>

7. Mina takes the newspaper. **but** She never reads it.
   ^

   <u>Mina takes the newspaper, but she never reads it.</u>

UNIT 6 A Changing America • **Lesson 4** *Martha Helps the Rebels*

Compound Sentences

Read the following sentences and put an arrow where the comma should be. Write the correct conjunction for joining the sentences over the arrow. Then copy the compound sentence correctly on the lines below.

and
1. Peter has a beagle⌃ Greg has a collie.

Peter has a beagle, and Greg has a collie.

or
2. Did you miss your doctor appointment?⌃ Was it canceled?

Did you miss your doctor appointment, or was it canceled?

and
3. Snow fell for days and days⌃ Skiers were very happy.

Snow fell for days and days, and skiers were very happy.

and
4. First the gymnasts warm up⌃ Then they compete.

First the gymnasts warm up, and then they compete.

but
5. I like to do crossword puzzles⌃ I never can finish them.

I like to do crossword puzzles, but I never can finish them.

and
6. Jenna painted a lovely picture⌃ Then she had it framed.

Jenna painted a lovely picture, and then she had it framed.

but
7. The dog is usually friendly⌃ He can be mean.

The dog is usually friendly, but he can be mean.

UNIT 6 A Changing America • **Lesson 5** *Going West*

Common Irregular Verbs

Read the following sentences, and circle the correct form of the irregular verb. Then copy the sentences correctly on the lines below.

1. The boys (are, (were)) late to dinner last night.

   The boys were late to dinner last night.

2. Please ((keep,) kept) the kitchen clean while I'm out.

   Please keep the kitchen clean while I'm out.

3. I really like the CD you (choose, (chose)).

   I really like the CD you chose.

4. My mom ((thinks,) thought) I have a great smile.

   My mom thinks I have a great smile.

5. This morning, Liz and I (speak, (spoke)) on the phone.

   This morning, Liz and I spoke on the phone.

6. It is time for the baby to ((sleep,) slept).

   It is time for the baby to sleep.

7. Paul wants to ((sell,) sold) his bike.

   Paul wants to sell his bike.

8. Every morning, at the bus stop, I ((stand,) stood) in line.

   Every morning, at the bus stop, I stand in line.

9. "Please ((forgive,) forgave) me," said Nina.

   "Please forgive me," said Nina.

Name _____ Date _____

Common Irregular Verbs

Read the following sentences and circle the correct form of the
irregular verb. Then copy the sentences correctly on the lines below.

1. The wind (blow, (blew)) loudly during the storm.

   The wind blew loudly during the storm.

2. I am trying to ((steal), stole) second base.

   I am trying to steal second base.

3. The tight end (catch, (caught)) the football and scored.

   The tight end caught the football and scored.

4. Drake and Melissa always ((know), knew) the right answers.

   Drake and Melissa always know the right answers.

5. Trent carefully (wind, (wound)) the bandage around my sprained ankle.

   Trent carefully wound the bandage around my

   sprained ankle.

6. It is time for us to ((eat), ate).

   It is time for us to eat.

7. Last summer, we (fly, (flew)) to Mexico for our vacation.

   Last summer, we flew to Mexico for our vacation.

8. Missy (lay, (laid)) the baby down in its crib.

   Missy laid the baby down in its crib.

9. When I walk the balance beam, I try not to ((fall), fell).

   When I walk the balance beam, I try not to fall.

10. My brother ((leaves), left) for college next month.

    My brother leaves for college next month.

UNIT 6   A Changing America • **Lesson 6** *The California Gold Rush*

Verbs: Past, Present, and Future Tenses

A *verb* is a word that tells about an action. It can tell about something that already happened *(past tense)*, something that is happening *(present tense)*, or something that will happen *(future tense)*. Underline the correct verb for the sentences in the following paragraphs.

There are many places to **visit visited** in a neighborhood. You can **mailed mail** letters at the post office. Cars and trucks will **stopped stop** at the gas station for fuel. I walk to the barber's shop and he **trims trimmed** my hair. At the bakery, I will **pick picked** up a fresh loaf of bread.

Dinosaurs **roam roamed** Earth long before people did. Many dinosaurs **live lived** near swamps. Plant-eaters **pluck plucked** leaves from the tops of trees. Meat-eaters **hunts hunted** alone or in packs. Some dinosaurs **soared soar** through the sky.

My family wants to **travel traveled** to Arizona this summer. I asked my dad whether we will **drive drives** there. He said he wants to stop along the way and see some sights that he **visit visited** when he was younger. My brother wants to **buy buys** a new camera to take pictures of the Grand Canyon. I know I will **like likes** this vacation!

UNIT 6 A Changing America • **Lesson 6** *The California Gold Rush*

Verbs: Past, Present, and Future Verbs

Read the story and underline each incorrect verb. Write the correct verb above it. Then write the story correctly on the lines below.

                saw   **were**

Last week Harry sees some birds. The birds are blue with tan chests.

     did   **looked**

Harry will not know what they were. The next day Harry looks in his bird

                         was   **were**

book. He found a picture of the birds. He is excited. They will be blue birds.

   learned   **looks**

He learns that blue birds are rare. Now Harry looked for birds each day. He

         see   **writes**

hopes he will saw another rare bird soon. Each day Harry wrote down the

kinds of birds he sees.

     Last week Harry saw some birds. The birds were blue with tan chests. Harry did not know what they were. The next day Harry looked in his bird book. He found a picture of the birds. He was excited. They were blue birds. He learned that blue birds are rare. Now Harry looks for birds each day. He hopes he will see another rare bird soon. Each day Harry writes down the kinds of birds he sees.

_____

_____

_____

_____

_____

_____

UNIT 6 A Changing America • **Lesson 7** *The Golden Spike*

Review Skill: Capitalization and End Punctuation

Read the story. Circle each word that should begin with a capital letter. Circle every end punctuation that is incorrect. Write the correct word or end punctuation above each circle. Then write the story correctly on the lines below.

    ,   **Where**   **?**

"Hey! wait for me?" yelled Danny. "where are you going!"

We

"we are going to see the monkeys," Matt answered.

I

"i want to go with you," said Danny.

Okay

"okay, come on," said Bill.

Standing   **After**

standing in front of the cage, the friends watched the monkeys. after a

while, one of the monkeys patted the other monkey on his back.

               ?

"Did you see that." asked John.

That

"that is one way they talk to each other," replied Matt?

_____"Hey! wait for me," yelled Danny. "Where are_____

you going?"

_____"We are going to see the monkeys," Matt answered._

_____"I want to go with you," said Danny._

_____"Okay, come on," said Bill._

_____Standing in front of the cage, the friends watched_

the monkeys. After a while, one of the monkeys patted

the other monkey on his back.

_____"Did you see that?" asked John._

_____"That is one way they talk to each other,"_

replied Matt.

UNIT 6   A Changing America • **Lesson 7** *The Golden Spike*

Review Skill: Capitalization and End Punctuation

Read the story. Circle each word that should begin with a capital letter. Circle every end punctuation that is incorrect. Write the correct word or end punctuation above each circle. Then write the story correctly on the lines below.

The
(the) town crier tells people to come to the fair. Where is the fair being
?
held(!) It is in Market Square(?) I ask my mother whether we can go(?) Wow,
! Merchants
there will be puppet shows, races, and tightrope walker(s.) (merchants) and

peddlers will bring their goods to the annual fair.
The
(the) town crier continues on his way, loudly asking people to come to
. Mother   I
the fair(!) (mother) and (i) go to the fair to see the merchants, peddlers, and the
?
live entertainment(?) What a great time!

_____The town crier tells people to come to the fair._____

_____Where is the fair being held? It is in Market Square. I_____

_____ask my mother whether we can go. Wow, there will be_____

_____puppet shows, races, and tightrope walkers!_____

_____Merchants and peddlers will bring their goods to the_____

_____annual fair._____

_____The town crier continues on his way, loudly asking_____

_____people to come to the fair. Mother and I go to the fair_____

_____to see the merchants, peddlers, and the live_____

_____entertainment. What a great time!_____

_____

_____